zhong
Earl Grey

tea clipper **Tea**
pluck

Assam **time**

green tea   fanning

Christian Manil
Marie Zbinden

CASSELL&CO

64%

of the world's tea is produced by India, China and Sri Lanka. India alone is responsible for *34%*, two-thirds of which it reserves for domestic consumption. China produces *19%*, Sri Lanka *11%*, Kenya *10%* and Japan *6%*.

The record for tea drinking goes to the Irish:

who consume 3.6 kg (7.92 lb) per person per year.

Next to water, tea is the most commonly consumed drink in the world.

It was in 2737 BC: the Emperor of China, Shen Nung, discovered the virtues of tea; it was slightly bitter in taste but rich in aroma.

is the highest price ever paid for tea.

32

The rarest teas cost between £150 and £6,000 per kilo. An authentic Dong Ding, of which 210 kg (462 lb) is produced annually, fetches around £9,000 per kilo. 32

Novelty teas of the 1990s:

*A plethora of tea is sold in cans, bottles and packets – it can be flavoured and served iced or sparkling.
Sales of these products were projected at **2,500 million** litres in Europe in 2000.*

32

It takes **four years** for a tea plant to be able to produce tea.

The oldest trees, ranging from **100 to 200 years old**, give the best yield.

The oldest tea tree in the world is **1,600 years old** and stands **30 m (98 ft)** tall !

56

Cha (pronounced *tcha*),
is the Chinese character for tea. Its medicinal properties have been
recognised for over 3,000 years in China.

 13

'Tea is nothing more than this:
heating water, making tea and drinking it.'
Sen No Rikyû, also known as Soeki (1522–91).

 18

In China, tea is served in small, fine porcelain cups with no
handles. It is drunk at any time of day.

 15

Tea houses, which were banned by Mao Tse Tung,
have recently reopened in China.
People go there to relax,
listen to a play, chat or eat.

 48

Multilingual tea

Te Chaya
Denmark   India

Tae Boeja
Israel   Tibet

Cha Tzai
Japan   Iran

Thee Té
Netherlands   Spain

Tèh Tchaï
Indonesia   Russia

Thé Tee
France   Germany

Containing no calories or sodium, **since ancient times tea has been recognised for its numerous qualities:** caffeine stimulates the nervous system and astringent tannins ease digestion. Tea boosts the circulation of blood, is good for the heart, prevents tooth decay and acts as a diuretic.

Tea can be combined

with essence of camellia, jasmine or rose, and with many flavours including lychee, chocolate, vanilla or caramel.

The flavour of tea depends on the receptacle used, and more importantly, the quality of the water.
Lu Yu recommended, in order of preference, mountain water, river water, and finally spring water.

The way tea is prepared
and drunk is influenced by the
various traditions prevalent in different
countries. **In Russia**, tea is strongly concentrated
and is served in glasses. People sometimes place a
lump of sugar in their mouths before drinking it.
The samovar has a reserve of boiling water so that
visitors can be offered a cup of traditional tea at any
time of day. **In Vietnam** tea is drunk from cups with
lids. **Arabian tea** is very sweet and infused with mint,
and is drunk from small glasses. **Japanese tea** is
drunk as part of an elaborate ceremony that
must be followed to the letter and requires
years of experience to perform.

'All you're supposed to do is every once in a while give the boys a little tea and sympathy.'
Tea and Sympathy, Act I

Robert Anderson

'When you taste English coffee, you realise why the English are fanatical drinkers of tea.'

Pierre Daninos in Les Carnets du Major Thomson

'Oh, my Friends, be warned by me, That Breakfast, Dinner, Lunch and Tea Are all the Human Frame requires'

Hilaire Belloc
'Henry King' Cautionary Tales

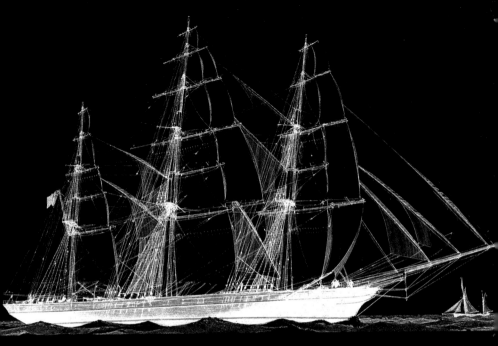

DISCOVER

FOLLOW TEA'S LONG JOURNEY FROM CHINA TO
JAPAN AND THEN ACROSS THE SEAS ABOARD THE
SHIPS OF THE EAST INDIA COMPANY. LEARN
HOW THIS HUMBLE BEVERAGE PROVOKED
BLOODY BATTLES IN EUROPE TO COUNTER
CHINESE SUPREMACY IN THE WORLD MARKET.

The origins of tea drinking are shrouded in the mysteries and legends of the East. According to Chinese tradition, tea was discovered by Emperor Shen Nung who ruled China many centuries ago and was known for his interest and forward thinking in medicine. He advised his subjects to boil their water before drinking it and scoured the countryside for new plants and healing remedies. The story goes that one day, in the year 2737 BC, feeling ill from trying out one of his new 'remedies', he sat down beneath the shade of a tea tree. Following his own advice he boiled some water to drink. As he did so some of the leaves from the tree blew into his cup. He drank the water nevertheless and found that it had acquired a rich aroma although with a slightly bitter taste. He soon began to feel better and became convinced of the therapeutic qualities of this new drink that he had discovered. The Japanese legend tells of an Indian prince, Bodhidharma, who went to China in the sixth century AD to found Chan Buddhism. He vowed never to fall asleep until his mission was accomplished. This vow proved difficult to keep, however, and exhausted, he fell asleep at the side of the road. When he woke, he pulled out his eyelashes to punish himself. A few years later, he returned to the same spot and found that two tea plants had grown where his eyelashes had fallen. According to Indian legend, the same prince, Bodhidharma, when advanced in years, had begun to meditate opposite a rock. After a while he grew tired and gathered some leaves that had fallen near the rock and chewed them. They gave him the strength to overcome his weariness and maintain his concentration and, thanks to this discovery, he managed to keep his vow not to sleep for nine years.

SHEN NUNG

According to legend, Emperor Shen Nung discovered tea and its therapeutic qualities in 2737 BC.

BOILED, WHISKED OR INFUSED – TEA IN CHINA

Legends aside, tea is said to have been used in Chinese medicine for over 3,000 years. For a long time, tea was taken as a food in the form of soup, in combination with other ingredients. However, where black tea is mentioned in ancient treatises (in the sixth and seventh centuries BC), it is in the form of the character *Tu*, which was the symbol for several bitter plants. Tea was subjected to taxation from the earliest times and played a key role in the history of China. It was during the Han dynasty (206 BC–220 AD) that tea began to be consumed as a drink, but since production was limited, tea drinking was a privilege afforded only to the court. It was also during this period that the character *Tu* was replaced by the character *Cha* to denote tea. Under the Nanbei dynasty (420–589 AD), Buddhism promoted first the cultivation then the distribution of tea. The monks valued tea for its stimulating qualities, as it helped them pray and meditate. Tea plantations developed around the most prestigious temples, new varieties appeared and propagation methods improved, as did the art of preparing tea, for which a code

of practice was gradually laid down. Lastly, tea began to be recognised for its therapeutic uses. At this time, tea was supplied compressed into blocks which were then heated to break them up. The leaves were reduced to a powder and diluted with hot water and the tea was often drunk boiling hot. Ingredients such as salt, spices and onion were added, and it was in this form, as a kind of soup, that it was introduced in around the sixth century into Tibet, where it is still drunk in this way today. During the sixth century tea was transported some 1,500 kilometres (931 miles) across China to Tibet and towards Mongolia, carried on the backs of camels and yaks. This trade provided the Chinese, who had no horses for their army, with the funds to buy them from Mongolia. Tea increased in popularity during the Tang dynasty (618–907AD), which was when the first teahouses appeared. Poets, potters and painters all contributed to making the art of tea drinking more sophisticated. In the eighth century, Lu Yu wrote the first treatise devoted to tea, *The Classic of Tea* (*Cha Ching*). It was under the Sung dynasties (960–1279) that tea began to appear in a loose form to satisfy popular demand. At the same time more ordinary varieties were produced, with the advantage that they could be manufactured more quickly and were easier to prepare. The teas that the court selected, in contrast, were becoming more and more refined. Tea bowls became shallower but wider and the tea was ground with stone into a fine powder, and a bamboo whisk was used to whisk this powder in the hot water into a delicate froth. This is the method of tea drinking that was introduced to Japan in the 12th century, and this is how it is still drunk there today during the tea ceremony, called *chanoyu* (literally 'hot water for tea'). The preparation of tea continued to evolve under the Ming dynasty (1368–1644), when the Emperor ordered the manufacture of compressed tea to be stopped, and the production of loose leaf tea began to expand. The tea-making method then began to change as the loose tea leaves were infused in the water rather than whisked. This triggered the appearance of kettles and teapots, made of clay or porcelain, as well as small cups without handles, and so the modern art of tea drinking was born. As for the tea trade, it was about to see a new boom with the arrival of the Dutch in China.

TEA SHOP

Between the 14th and 17th centuries the production and trade of loose tea saw an unprecedented boom in China.

LU YU AND THE 'CLASSIC OF TEA'

A poet and philosopher of the Tang period, Lu Yu was also one of the great tea masters. Orphaned as a child, he was taken into a monastery by a Zen master, who gave him his name (Lu means 'great land' and Yu 'feathers'), but he didn't want to become a monk and ran away with a troop of travelling performers. He settled in the province of Zhejiang where he devoted himself to his work until he retired, dying at the age of 81 in 804AD. Around 780, he published

The Classic of Tea (Cha Ching), which was to influence not only his contemporaries but also great tea masters to come. In this book he describes the origin, history, plantation, production, preparation and consumption of tea. There are references to the fine porcelain whose production had been perfected two centuries earlier, but the wares deemed most suitable for drinking tea were greenish-grey celadons. Lu Yu wrote in some detail of the best method of drinking tea: 'There is no simple method. Simply picking tea in the shade and drying it in the cool of the evening is not what I call producing tea... Reducing it to a jade powder or green dust is not grinding tea. Using utensils awkwardly and switching from one to the other thus attracting attention is no way to make tea.'

Lu Tung, another aesthete, described as 'mad about tea', said: 'Immortality means nothing to me at all – all I am interested in is the taste of tea.' He dedicated his life to the practice of tea drinking, applying both the Taoist theory of 'non-action' and Confucius' cherished principles of ritual and moderation.

TEA IN JAPAN

Two centuries after the commercialisation of Chinese tea in Tibet in the seventh century AD, the Korean ambassador in China procured a tea plant from the Tang court and returned with it to his country. This plant is said to be the origin of the vast plantations in South Korea. There is little to choose between this tea and the best of the Chinese yields, but it was from the Koreans that the Japanese adopted the term *Cha* as the word for tea when it was introduced in Japan under the aegis of the monks.

THE TEA CEREMONY

It was in the 16th century that Sen No Rikyū devised the rules for the tea ceremony.

At the beginning of the ninth century, the Buddhist monk Saicho (also known as Dengyo Daishi) planted the first tea seeds at the foot of his monastery at Sakamoto. It was the first Japanese tea garden. Some years later in Saga, another monk, Eichu, offered the Emperor a tea he had prepared himself. The Emperor was so impressed that he saw to it that new plantations were established. However, when the commercial treaties with China expired in 894, tea went out of fashion. It was not until the 12th century when the Zen Buddhist Eisai brought back new seeds from China that the method of drinking tea as a whisked powder was introduced. He promised that it would be available to all Japanese people, but it was not until 1654 that a Chinese monk finally introduced the tea infusion method known as *Sencha*.

FROM A SIMPLE BEVERAGE TO THE TEA CEREMONY

No doubt it was the close links between Buddhism and the introduction of tea in Japan that led to the ritualisation of tea drinking. However, even though it began as an aid to meditation, it soon also became a therapeutic drink and then an excuse for socialising, whether at the court or among the samurai, who organised various competitions including blindfold tea tastings. Thus the art of tea drinking came to have spiritual, therapeutic and social elements, and has been moulded by successive influences. Eisai had laid the foundations for its usage, the monk Murata Shukô and the learned merchant Takeno Jo-o nurtured the 'way of tea' (*sado*), while Sen No Rikyû, also called Soeki (1522–1591), created a whole philosophy around the tea ceremony or *chanoyu*. The idea was that the ceremony should function as the ultimate celebration of the four Taoist virtues of purity, harmony, respect and wisdom. It was performed according to a strict set of rules that combined religion with diplomacy. Rikyû became an important figure, and established the 'seven secrets of the way of tea' that govern the preparation of the ceremony:

> *Make a delicious bowl of tea*
> *Arrange the charcoal so that it can heat the water*
> *Arrange the flowers as they are in the field*
> *Evoke coolness in summer and warmth in winter*
> *Do everything ahead of time*
> *Be prepared for rain even if it is not raining*
> *Pay the utmost attention to each of your guests*

A WAY OF LIFE
The fashion for infused tea, known as Sencha, became established in Japan from the 17th century onwards.

His entire philosophy, which was to influence masters of the tea ceremony throughout the centuries, is summed up quite simply in the following few words: 'Tea is nothing more than this: heating water, making tea, and drinking it.' Sen No Rikyû is one of the most outstanding figures of Japanese cultural history, one whose influence has extended down through the ages. After him his sons and grandsons carried on the tradition, and even today, his descendants are to be found as directors of tea schools.

TEA ARRIVES IN EUROPE

The first mention of tea in the West is by an Arab merchant who wrote about it in his work *Relations of China and India* in 851. The tales of great voyagers criss-crossing Asia with plants and seeds fire the imagination, but it wasn't until the 17th century that Europe finally discovered tea, when Jesuit missionaries brought back the first tea leaves from China. Portugal gained control of the coasts of Africa, Arabia, India and Indonesia and in 1577, Portuguese merchants founded Macao, opposite Canton. The Dutch started to buy tea directly from the

Chinese importing it from Macao. The first cargos were unloaded at Amsterdam in 1606 by the Dutch East India Company, which retained the monopoly on the tea trade until 1669. Gradually, the Dutch and the Danish became great consumers of tea.

Tea officially arrived in England via the court in the mid-17th century. The appearance of the first coffee houses helped its distribution and increased its popularity. Reserved for men only, these establishments served coffee or tea with cakes and pastries. In 1706, tea became valued on its own merit when Thomas Twining opened the first tea room in

London, which was called *Tom's Coffee House*. He offered tea in cups and, most importantly, opened his doors to female clientele. From then on the usage of tea became widespread throughout the British Isles. The custom of serving afternoon tea with cakes was begun by the Duchess of Bedford around 1840.

It was via Holland that tea found its way into France under Louis XIII in 1636 but it was only drunk by the aristocracy. In 1693, Frenchman Philippe Sylvestre Dufour published his *Treatise on Tea*, which reflected the enthusiasm of the European upper classes for the new drink and was packed with precious information on its usage and preparation according to ancient Chinese tradition. An exclusive and highly expensive product, tea remained the privilege of the aristocracy for almost two centuries before first the bourgeoisie and then the literary and fashionable salons discovered its appeal too.

In 1854, Henri and Edouard Mariage founded the Parisian teahouse Mariage Frères but it wasn't until the early 1900s that French tea drinking became more widespread and the first salons de thé sprang up in Paris, followed by a number of provincial towns and seaside resorts in northern France.

BRITISH SUPREMACY IN THE TEA TRADE

From 1615 the East India Company, British rival of the Dutch East India Company, began to show an interest in tea, but it wasn't until the end of the 1660s, when the government prohibited the Dutch from importing their tea into Britain, that it started to trade with China. In 1638 Japan closed its ports to the West, cutting itself off for more than two centuries. This meant that only China was able to provide tea to the Dutch. But the Chinese hounded them out of Formosa (Taiwan), and the British company was quick to seize the opportunity this presented. In 1669, the East India Company's first cargo of tea was unloaded in London, and the ensuing monopoly was to last for over a century.

As the trade in tea rocketed, so did the taxes. From 1660, tea sold in cafés and taverns was hit by a tax that remained in force until 1689, by which time a pound of ordinary tea would cost the

average English worker a week's wages. This tax was replaced by a new import tax, but even more excessive taxes followed which meant that smuggling increased and flourished. Between 50 per cent and 75 per cent of tea was imported illegally. This made tea more accessible to the working classes, even if its quality was poor. In 1784, taxes were reduced and official consumption rose from 65 kg (143 lb) in 1699, to 2 tonnes (4,400 lb) in 1769, 30 tonnes (66,000 lb) in 1701 and 6,800 tonnes (14,960,000 lb) in 1791.

Economically, there was a lot at stake – the supply of this particular manna from heaven had to be maintained. The East India Company took the helm and in 1684 managed to set up a British trading post in Canton. In no time at all, tea came to represent 90 per cent of Chinese imports to England. But there was a heavy price to pay: China demanded commission, refused to import British textiles and closed access to other ports. The British, affronted by this treatment, decided to swamp the Chinese market with opium imported from their trading posts in India, which provided a useful exchange currency. Although opium was already being produced and consumed in the province of Sichuan, its usage became more widespread when combined with tobacco. Not only the Chinese economy but also its society were to suffer from this trade. The British colony of India, however, prospered thanks to the increased sales of home-grown poppies.

THE CARAVAN ROUTE

Meanwhile, another tea route was emerging. In 1689, the border between Russia and China was defined in the treaty of Nerchinsk, allowing trading caravans to move between the two countries. At last, a land route was open. It took caravans of 200 to 300 camels leaving Moscow six months to reach the Chinese border at Kietha (or Kiakhta), a small town of 5,000 inhabitants where a great trade fair was organised in December for Russians and Chinese to meet and trade fur and tea. The camels were then loaded up again for the six-month journey back to Moscow. Because of the journey the tea was already one and a half years old before it reached the table. In 1817, a second trade fair opened at Nijni-Novgorod, which took place in July. The journey between Kietha and this great river port at the confluence of the Volga and the Oka rivers took two years by land or three years by inland waterway. As in Europe the high price of tea meant that it was drunk exclusively by the aristocracy but annual consumption had increased dramatically by 1800. The number of camels in the caravans rose from 600 in 1700 to over 6,000 in 1800.

SAMOVAR

In Russia in the 19th century, the exorbitant price of tea meant it was reserved for the aristocracy.

Russia exported tea to Sweden, Denmark and what is now northern Germany. With Chinese ports now open to Russian ships and, at the turn of the 20th century, the Trans-Siberian railway

in operation, tea transportation time was reduced to just a few days, dealing a fatal blow to the caravans.

UNREST IN THE NEW WORLD

In 1647, the Dutchman Peter Stuyvesant arrived in America and made his fortune from trading tea in the large coastal towns of the 13 colonies of New England. The American 'tea civilisation' was about to be born. Over the years, the elite held tea parties in New York, Philadelphia and Boston, and Americans found they simply couldn't do without their tea. This need was cleverly fuelled by the British East India Company, even though most of the tea exported to New York was Dutch contraband. In 1773, the company obtained a monopoly on tea trade in the colonies from the British government. From then on, it could pick and choose its American buyers and as a result, many were barred from the official system and joined the growing ranks of contraband merchants and malcontents. To fill the coffers depleted by the Thirty Years War, the British Crown had already imposed a new tax on the import of tea into its American colony in 1767 (the Townsend Act), which had caused widespread ill feeling. A campaign to boycott British tea was soon established.

BOSTON TEA PARTY

On the 16 December 1773, the townspeople of Boston, disguised as Indians, hurled a cargo of English tea into the sea.

At this time, tea was the third major product imported by America, after textiles and manufactured goods. The 1773 Tea Act, which contained new customs laws, was the final straw. On 16 December, dozens of armed men disguised as Indians (thought to be members of an influential Masonic lodge close to Benjamin Franklin) descended on Boston harbour, attacking the three ships which were unloading their goods and hurling 342 chests of tea into the sea. This event became known as the Boston Tea Party. Hostile feeling was increased when London imposed repressive laws and acts of American patriotism against the British followed in retaliation. The War of Independence loomed.

THE OPIUM WARS: 1840–42 AND 1856–60

During this period, the Chinese were also at the receiving end of Britain's coercive measures. While opium made the British Empire rich, it was ruining China. China resolved to take action and in 1800 it banned the import of opium. The traffickers soon found a way round this – instead of unloading the opium at Canton, they landed it on an island opposite the port. In June 1839, the Emperor sent a special envoy to seize and burn 20,000 smuggled cases of the drug. Britain went on the offensive, launching a series of military operations between 1840 and 1842 that became known as 'the first opium war'. This was ended by the treaty of Nanking when

China ceded Britain the island of Hong Kong, permitted access to the ports of Canton, Shanghai, Ningbo, Amoy and Fuzhou, and reduced customs rates to 5 per cent. Foreign residents were beyond Chinese jurisdiction. After some years, faced with what they considered the hostility of the Chinese, the British declared war in 1856. This was the 'second opium war' and this time the French took part in the conflict and the town of Peking was pillaged. In 1860, the treaty of Tianjin was signed, opening 11 new Chinese ports to foreign trade and allowing missionaries access to the Chinese interior. Foreign delegations were permitted to enter the Chinese capital and war ships could use the waterways. Opium trade became illegal once more but by 1878, 120 million Chinese were opium addicts. British domination of the Middle Kingdom had been well and truly established.

CLIPPERS – THE WEAPONS OF TRADE

As long as the East India Company had a monopoly on the transport of tea to Britain, the speed of the ships was not a significant factor, even though six months at sea affected the quality of this delicate cargo. The company preferred to transport tea on short, wide ships called Indiamen. Although they were slow, they were short enough to be exempt from British tax, which was determined according to the length of the boat.

In 1834, the British decided to put an end to the East India Company's monopoly and the Americans took the opportunity to penetrate the British market. Now that competition was possible, the top priority was to become first on the market, especially since the opening of the Chinese port at Fuzhou, which was closer to the main plantations than Canton, made it possible to trade with tea made from the first crops of the year. Known as first crop leaves, these plentiful, high-quality crops were greatly

THE THERMOPYLAE
The advent of clippers in the 19th century revolutionised the transport of tea by sea.

sought after by tea lovers. It was at this time that the first clippers, as the American sailing ships were known, appeared on the scene. Clippers were fast, sleek ships with enormous sails, their name referring to the way they cut through the waves. The very first of these ships, *Rainbow*, embarked on its maiden voyage in 1845. The high cost of its construction was recouped in the single trip from New York to Hong Kong. In 1850, the clipper *Oriental* became the first American vessel to enter the port of London. She had left Hong Kong 95 days previously, shortening the usual duration of the voyage by two weeks. Her cargo of tea was the first on the market and her owners, with no competition to worry about, made a substantial profit.

It wasn't long before the British decided to build their own clippers and a battle of speed between the Americans and the British ensued. Of comparable speed, British tea clippers were subjected to relentless voyages across the oceans, however, one of the most famous, the Cutty

Sark, can be seen at Greenwich. The opening of the Suez Canal in 1869 and the arrival of steam boats marked the beginning of the end for clippers.

WHY IMPORT WHEN YOU CAN PRODUCE?

Tea was a great source of profit for those in the trade, but why import it at great expense when there was the option of producing it yourself? In the 18th century, Europeans dreamed of being able to acclimatise and grow this precious plant at home. However, first the botanists needed to get hold of the seeds to learn about their cultivation, but this was a secret the Chinese had no intention of sharing. The botanist Linné in Sweden was the first to attempt to grow tea, but the Scandinavian climate was hardly suitable for cultivating tea plants. Meanwhile early endeavours by the Dutch at growing tea in Java also ended in failure and the French fared no better when they tried to grow tea plants at Finistère in Brittany.

It was the British who eventually managed to get it right – not because of any superior skill but thanks to the extent of their colonial reach as the tea plant could be cultivated outside China, but it needed a warmer climate than European latitudes could provide.

A TENTATIVE START FOR INDIA

During the 18th century, Britain's commercial relations with China were not good. Under the Treaty of Paris (which brought the Seven Years' War to an end in 1763) French territory in India, as well as Canada, was given over to Britain. British colonisation intensified along with the cultivation and trade of tea. In 1788, the botanist Joseph Bank succeeded in transporting Chinese tea plants to Calcutta, where some managed to acclimatise. This in itself was not enough to make

PICKING TEA

In 1848, Robert Fortune scoured China for the secrets of tea cultivation.

the East India Company enter into the business of cultivation, as it still lacked the expertise. However, the conquest of Assam in 1834 enabled Major Robert Bruce to discover vast expanses of tea plants growing wild in this northern region of India. Now was the time to learn the means and methods that had until now been the exclusive domain of the Chinese, and uncover the mysteries of tea. To this end, the governor of India created the Tea Committee in 1834 that was to send emissaries to appropriate the secret of the Middle Kingdom. The committee's official role was to study all aspects of tea plantation, production and trade.

THE ADVENTURES OF ROBERT FORTUNE

The committee's most pressing objective, however, was to set up a daring espionage operation, which was entrusted to the Scottish botanist Robert Fortune in 1848. His mission was to go to

China on Her Majesty's service, shaven and disguised as a Manchu. He had travelled to China before, but this time his mission was to steal the secrets of tea production. He left Shanghai in a sedan chair and made his way onto tea farms where he collected seeds with great care and sent them off to the botanic gardens of Calcutta and London. He kept a detailed journal containing all the information he acquired relating to the cultivation and production of tea, including the valuable advice a Buddhist monk gave him on the importance of water quality when infusing the leaves. After an eventful trip, he returned to Calcutta with 80 Chinese factory owners and 20,000 tea plants, which were to be distributed throughout India. Europeans had finally penetrated the mysteries of tea cultivation.

INDIA, ASSAM AND CEYLON

In 1820, General Lloyd discovered the site of Darjeeling, whose name means 'place of thunderbolts' in Tibetan. Wild tea plants were found growing in the region which lay in the foothills of the Himalayas on the borders of Nepal, Tibet and India. In 1835, the British annexed Darjeeling, and the first tea tree plantations appeared there in 1856.

Robert Bruce having died, his brother, Charles Alexander Bruce, managed to set up experimental plantations in the jungle of Upper Assam. He began by clearing the area, then built the first Indian factories (as the processing buildings were called) and in 1836 delivered the first Assam tea to Calcutta. The year 1839 saw the first sales of Assam tea in London, where it was well received as its taste was more distinctive than that of China tea. Following this success, the Assam Company was founded. It proceeded systematically to create land for cultivation in the region and commercialise it.

TEA MANUFACTURE

The first tea factories appeared in India in the second half of the 19th century.

New plantation businesses were set up in many regions including Cachar, Dooars, Terai and Nilgiri. Ceylon (which gained independence in 1948 and, became Sri Lanka in 1972) was originally planted with coffee bushes. From 1825 the phenomenal growth of the coffee trade brought great riches to 'Ceylon'. But these plantations were devastated by rust between 1865 and 1890, after which there was virtually no coffee left growing on the island. Attempts had already been made at growing tea in 1860, but now the production of tea was poised to supplant that of coffee. The first cargo was recorded in 1872 and by 1907 tea plants covered 150,000 hectares (370,500 acres). Britain's gamble had paid off.

A WORLD-WIDE INSTITUTION

Victorian Britain was accustomed to taking tea in the afternoon, along with a light meal, and this custom was soon established in the workplace. Tea time or five o'clock tea became an institution. More and more tea houses sprang up, offering scones, muffins, crumpets and cake to satisfy their clients' appetites. By 1887, imports of tea from British colonies were greater than those from China.

Nowadays, India remains the biggest exporter of tea in the world (34 per cent), followed by China (19 per cent), Sri Lanka (11 per cent) and Kenya (10 per cent), and then Indonesia, Pakistan and Taiwan. In 1981, world production of tea amounted to 1,845,000 tonnes (2,033,000 tons), of which more than 1,450,000 tonnes (1,598,000 tons) came from Asia alone. Next to water, tea is the most popular drink in the world. Ireland holds the tea-drinking record, with 3.6 kg (7.92 lb) of tea per head per year, followed by Britain, New Zealand and Canada. In mainland Europe, on the other hand, the Germans drink a mere 1 kg (2.2 lb) while the French can barely manage 230 g (8 oz), although this is on the increase.

TEA FOR ALL TASTES

It was the Tibetans that first set the trend for adapting tea by adding butter and salt to it and as early as the 19th century the Scandinavians were drinking tea mixed in equal proportions with Bordeaux, whilst the Russians added vodka to theirs. Tea can be used in the preparation of various cocktails with cordial (strawberry, raspberry or grenadine) or fruit juice (orange, lemon or pineapple), with spices (cinnamon, cloves, nutmeg or ginger), or with rum, champagne, cognac, and so forth, for alcoholic variations. It can also be drunk iced. The beginning of the 1990s saw the market flooded with a plethora of cans, bottles and packets of tea in all its guises – flavoured, iced, and sparkling. Sales of these products were projected at 2,500 million litres in Europe in 2000, which proves that when it comes to tea, novelty competes strongly with the purest of traditions.

It wasn't until the end of the 20th century that European consumers realised that there were such things as vintage teas. In fact, there are more vintage teas than there are vintage wines. There are several thousands of tea names, 1,500 of which apply to green tea alone. Production of some rare teas may be limited to 300 kg (660 lb), 6 kg (13.2 lb), or in the case of the Bai Hao in 1995, a mere 50 g (2 oz) per annum. Clearly, the price of these teas is determined by their rarity. Top vintages are sold for between £150 and £6,000 per kilo. An authentic Dong Ding, of which only 210 kg (462 lb) is produced, can fetch £9,000 per kilo.*

*These figures are taken from the book by Dominique T. Pasqualini, Le Temps du thé, pub. Marval, 1999.

LOOK

FROM LONDON TO BEIJING, FROM PAKISTAN TO RAJASTHAN, TEA TIME IS AN INSTITUTION AND SOMETIMES A SACRED AND RESPECTED OCCASION. THIS COLLECTION OF IMAGES GIVES AN INSIGHT INTO THE FINER POINTS OF TEA TRADITIONS AROUND THE WORLD.

'A photograph which allows no distance

6 PM, FRANCE

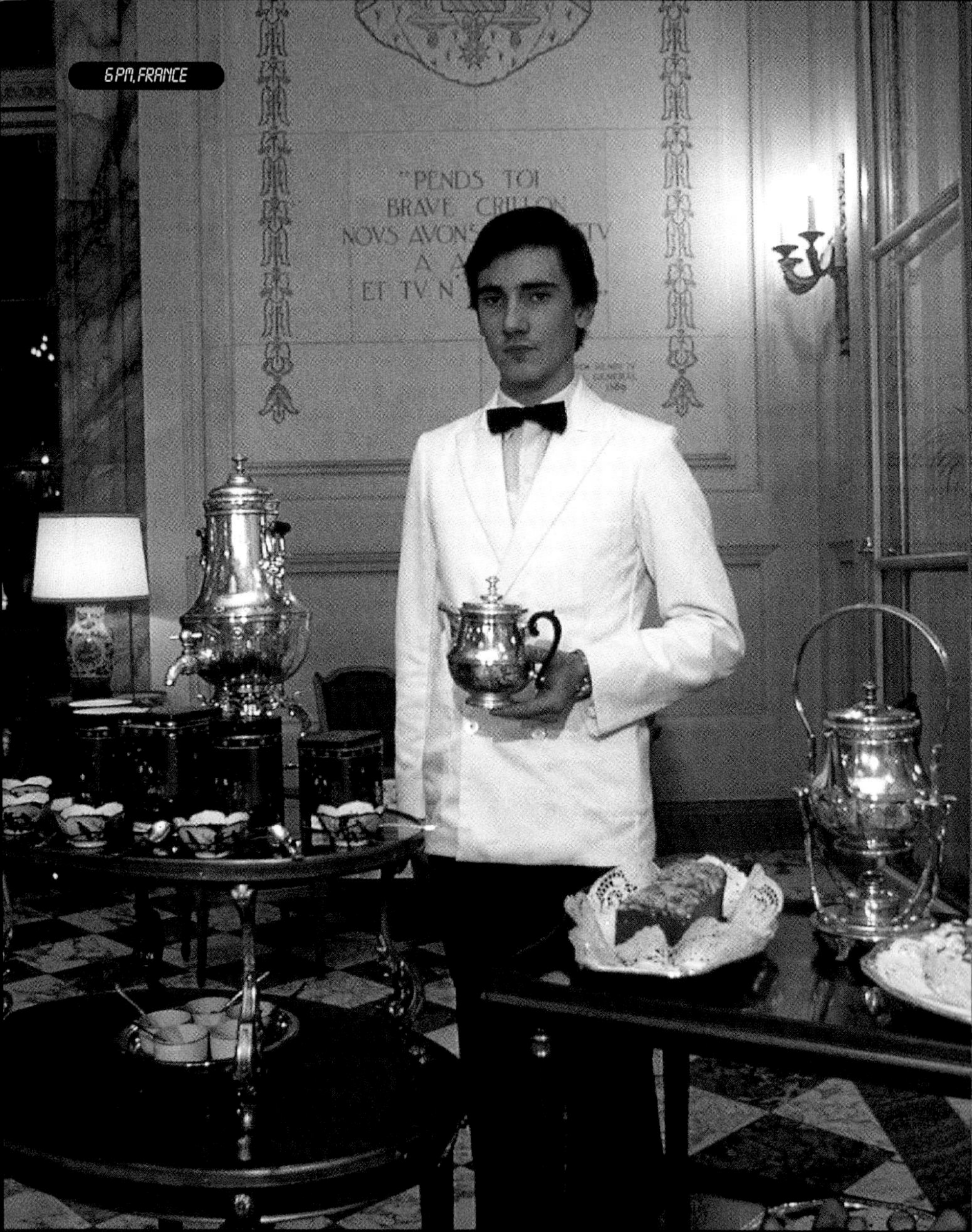

A picture of yellow and black

And the desert. Rocks piled low, Blue pot overturned

—a table. Cup with flower pattern. Cinders

A fire in the foreground almost hidden,

S.P.M. TUNISIA

And a woman with teapot held high, Face hidden,

Pouring tea from where she sits   Cross-legged in the desert

Into my cup where I sit

On a stool in my kitchen   In the city.

3 P.M., IRAQ

Such kindness allows no distance.'

Dave Ettel, *In Search of a Touareg Woman Pouring Tea*

IN PRACTICE

GREEN TEA, BLACK TEA, DARJEELING, YUNNAN – WHICH
SHOULD YOU CHOOSE? HOW DO YOU BEST INFUSE THE
LEAVES AND STORE THE TEA? WHAT KIND OF TEAPOT IS
PREFERABLE? TEA IS GOOD FOR YOUR HEALTH, SO WHY
NOT USE IT IN YOUR COOKING?

How to grow a tea plant

The tea plant is an evergreen shrub that belongs to the same order as the Guttiferae. It is a member of the Theaceae family and its genus is *Camellia*.

IT TAKES FOUR YEARS FOR A TEA PLANT TO BE ABLE TO PRODUCE TEA. THE OLDEST TEA PLANTS (100-200 YEARS OLD) PRODUCE THE BEST CROP.

One species but many estates

The tea plant is cultivated in plantations called 'estates', which can be small family-run concerns or can be as large as 1,000 hectares (2,470 acres).

In the wild, it can reach a height of 15 metres (50 feet), and the variety found in Assam, in India, can grow almost 20 metres (65 feet) tall. Today, only one *species* is cultivated – the *Camellia sinensis* but it has many varieties (almost 260 are grown in China). In 1843, Scottish botanist Robert Fortune discovered that green and black teas came from the same plant and simply differed in the way they were treated.

Pruning and plucking

The tea plant has a productive life of around 50 years, sometimes more. It needs pruning two or three times to make the trunk strong and, once it starts producing leaves, it must be pruned again several times in order for it to grow to its optimum height – about one metre – for plucking. Plucking is the term used for picking the leaves of the tea plant, and a pluck is the term used to describe the harvest of a particular crop.

Climate and altitude

Tea grows well in acidic soils in hot and humid regions (with at least 1,500 mm (60 in) of rain per annum). It is particularly suited to areas of high altitude (up to 2,500 metres, 8,200 feet) situated between 43 degrees north and 27 degrees south, where the days are hot and the nights are cool.

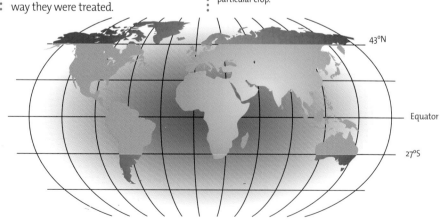

43°N

Equator

27°S

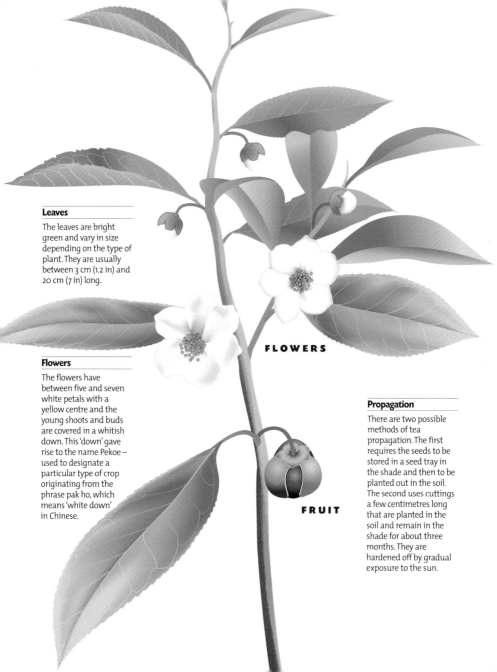

Leaves

The leaves are bright green and vary in size depending on the type of plant. They are usually between 3 cm (1.2 in) and 20 cm (7 in) long.

Flowers

The flowers have between five and seven white petals with a yellow centre and the young shoots and buds are covered in a whitish down. This 'down' gave rise to the name Pekoe – used to designate a particular type of crop originating from the phrase pak ho, which means 'white down' in Chinese.

FLOWERS

Propagation

There are two possible methods of tea propagation. The first requires the seeds to be stored in a seed tray in the shade and then to be planted out in the soil. The second uses cuttings a few centimetres long that are planted in the soil and remain in the shade for about three months. They are hardened off by gradual exposure to the sun.

FRUIT

A matter of quality

Tea is harvested in the same way all over the world, be it China, India or anywhere else. It is the young shoots and unopened leaf buds at the end of the branches that contain the most caffeine, tannins, vitamins and minerals and have the most delicate flavour.

In India

The first harvest is known as the first flush and takes place between 15 March and 15 May. This is not copious, but it is of fine quality. The lower leaves, close to the trunk, are bigger and less valuable. This harvest produces light teas that are rich in aroma. The second flush produces high-quality teas that make their way into European tea shops towards the end of October (which is the best time to buy them). The leaves produced from the third flush do not look as good, but their quality is still acceptable.

In China

There are three main harvests. The first takes place in spring and is known as the first crop. It is the best and most abundant. It is followed by the second crop and the third crop, which are of lower quality.

These crops may be blended but it is possible to find Chinese teas produced from the first crop alone.

Imperial pluck
(P + 1)

This harvest, no longer in use, involved the part of the stem comprising the bud at the tip (pekoe or P) and one leaf. Originally destined for use by the Emperor of China and certain high dignitaries, it had to be harvested by young virgins, who would use gold scissors to cut the stem without touching it, letting it fall into a golden basket.

Fine pluck
(P + 2)

This crop involves the bud at the tip and two leaves. It is the best quality tea found on the market today.

Coarse pluck
(P + 3)

For this crop, the bud and three leaves are taken. It is the most common type of crop and is of medium quality.
Including four leaves or more is possible, (P+4) but the quality of such a crop is very poor.

Picking tea leaves in Sumatra.

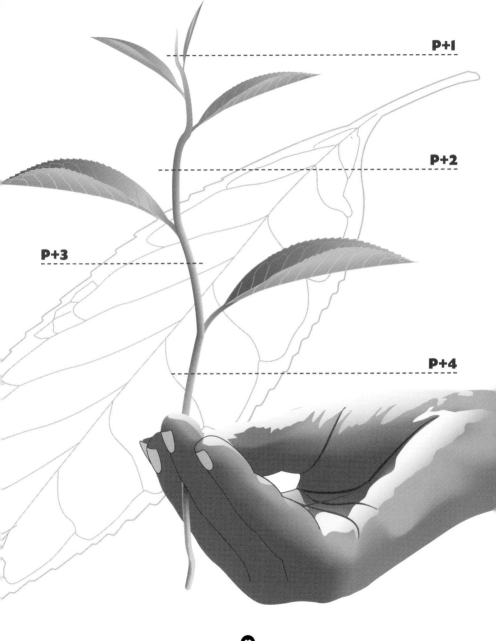

P+1

P+2

P+3

P+4

The metamorphosis of tea

Once harvested, the leaves of the tea plant are processed in factories often built on the plantation itself. It is during this process that the different types acquire their characteristics and personality. Oolong teas, for instance, are only slightly fermented, and green teas are unfermented.

FERMENTATION

The leaf now undergoes a series of complex chemical reactions that cause it to blacken. The process involves leaving the leaf in a humid environment (90–95 per cent) at a constant temperature (22°C), and allowing it to be oxidised by enzymes. If it is fermented too much, it loses its astringent character and the leaf looks burnt; if it is not fermented enough, it has a bitter taste and the leaf turns a greenish brown.

WITHERING

This process softens the leaf and allows it to lose between 40 and 50 per cent of its moisture. It usually lasts between 18 and 20 hours.

ROLLING

3

The leaves then pass through machines that roll them lengthways, breaking the cells and releasing their essential oils.

DRYING

4

This is a delicate operation that stops the fermentation process at the required moment. The leaves are subjected to a dry atmosphere and a high temperature that will conserve only 2–3 per cent of moisture.

GRADING

5

In the final step, the leaves are placed on vibrating sieve trays that sort them by grade (whole, broken, fanning – the very small fragments of leaf remaining after processing whole and broken leaves and so on) and by size. The tea is then wrapped in paper bags or placed in wooden crates lined with aluminium foil.

BRICK TEA

Compressing tea into bricks, cakes or 'birds' nests' is a Chinese tradition. Bricks are made from either compacted tea dust or from whole leaves. This is how it was transported on the backs of, camels on the caravan routes to Tibet and Russia, where this form of tea is still used today. Brick tea can also be bought in specialist tea shops in other countries. To make the tea small pieces of the brick are broken off and boiled in water for three to four minutes.

White, green and black

Teas are labelled according to their Western classification, which is based on the colour of their leaves after processing, the degree of fermentation, and the grade, which describes the shape and size of the leaf. Most are a blend of different teas, unlike pure teas, which come from a single estate. These pure teas are also called 'vintage teas'.

Green teas

These teas are unfermented – the natural fermentation process having been stopped. The Chinese throw freshly plucked leaves into a copper basin heated to almost 100°C. The Japanese, the other great producers of green tea, steam the leaves in a tank and roll them by hand.

CHINESE GREEN TEA

JAPANESE GREEN TEA

KENYAN BLACK TEA

CHINESE BLACK TEA

Black teas

These teas undergo different stages of fermentation to accelerate the transformation of the leaves to make them turn black.

Semi-fermented teas

Slotting in between the green and black teas, semi-fermented teas are known as Oolong ('black dragon' in Chinese). In China, they are reputed to possess the most desirable qualities. There are two types of fermentation. The first takes place at a humidity level of 10–15 per cent, producing teas that are more green than black and originated in China. The second method is practised in Taiwan, at a humidity level of 60–70 per cent, and produces teas that are more black than green. Highly prized, *Oolong* teas have the scent of green tea and the flavour of black tea.

LAPSANG SOUCHONG

ASSAM

White tea acquires its name from the colour of the leaf on the bush – a silvery white – and the white down on its bud. Rare and coming from the province of Fujian in China it is a natural tea that is simply withered and dried. There are two varieties: *Yin Zhen* (silver needle) and *Pai mu tan* (white peony).

DARJEELING

WHITE TEA

OOLONG

Grades of black tea

Black teas are divided into three main categories: whole leaf, broken leaf and fanning.

Whole leaf teas

Flowery Orange Pekoe (FOP) is produced from a high-quality crop. Its leaves twist lengthways and are about 6 mm (2.4 in) long.

Golden Flowery Orange Pekoe (GFOP) is an FOP with leaf buds and golden tips. *Tippy Golden Flowery Orange Pekoe* (TGFOP) is an FOP with many golden tips. *Finest Tippy Golden Flowery Orange Pekoe* (FTGFOP) is an FOP of extremely high quality.

Orange Pekoe (OP) is produced from a later crop of high quality leaves that are long and pointed, slightly bigger than the those of the FOP, twisted lengthways, but without buds. Since the final tip has by this time opened into a leaf, there are very few tips.

Flowery Pekoe (FP) has tightly rolled leaves that produce a full-flavoured tea.

Pekoe (P) has leaves that are shorter, of poorer quality than the OP, and have no tips. *Pekoe Souchong* (PS), with short, coarse leaves, has little aroma. *Souchong* (S) has large leaves twisted lengthways. Low in caffeine, it is sold as smoked Chinese tea.

Fanning teas

These teas are made of very small pieces of leaf. They have a fuller flavour and are sometimes used for tea bags, though less frequently than broken teas. They are classified in the same way: *Golden Orange Fanning* (GOF), *Flowery Orange Fanning* (FOF), *Orange Fanning* (OF), and *Pekoe Orange Fanning* (POF).

Broken teas

Broken teas are not of inferior quality. The term arises from the technique of breaking the whole leaves. Broken leaves have a greater surface area in contact with the water so the tea has a fuller flavour. One example is *Broken Orange Pekoe* (BOP).

Flowery Orange Pekoe

FOP

Golden Flowery Orange Pekoe

GFOP

Tippy Golden Flowery Orange Pekoe

TGFOP

Finest Tippy Golden Flowery Orange Pekoe

FTGFOP

Pekoe

P

Flowery Orange Fanning

FOF

Orange Pekoe

OP

Broken Orange Pekoe

BOP

Orange Fanning

OF

Flowery Pekoe

FP

Golden Orange Fanning

GOF

Pekoe Orange Fanning

POF

DUST TEAS

These teas are finer than Fanning, and are generally used for tea bags. The use of the word 'dust' does not mean that the tea is poor; it is simply the name given to the method of preparation. In fact, there are some excellent vintages under the designations Fanning and Dust.

CTC TEAS

These teas have undergone the processes of crushing, tearing, and curling. Once reserved for the coarser leaves from *Assam*, this procedure is now applied to quality leaves and produces attractively coloured teas. It is becoming a frequently used process.

Grades of green tea

Green tea is graded under the following categories: Gunpowder, Natural Leaf, Chun-Mee and Matcha.

Gunpowder

Gunpowder is produced from the first crop. The young leaves are selected and rolled into pellets the size of a pinhead – up to 3 mm (0.1 in) in diameter – which makes them resemble gunpowder. It is an excellent green tea.

Matcha

Matcha is a green tea (a *Gyokuro* or a *Sencha*) that has been reduced to a powder. The leaves are dried and then steamed so that they can be cut into pieces. They are then dried again and stoneground into a powder, a process which gives the tea its strong, bitter taste. Used by the Japanese in the tea ceremony (*chanoyu*), it is whisked into a jade-coloured froth. Only a small quantity is needed: approximately 1 g (0.035 oz) for six 10 cl (3.5 fl oz) cups of water heated to 60–70°C.

Chun-Mee

Chun-Mee is an excellent tea made of leaves that are between 8 mm (0.3 in) and 12 mm (0.4 in) long and twisted lengthways.

Natural Leaf

Natural Leaf comes from China and Japan. As the name implies, the leaf is left in its natural state – whole, which makes the tea very mild.

Green tea in Japan

Japan, which ranks seventh among the world's tea producers, now only manufactures green tea, 97 per cent of which is consumed within the country. The tea is cultivated in the southern region of the main island of Honchu and on the islands of Shikoku and Kyūshū, mainly at high altitude. Tea plants, which have a high resistance to the cold, are farmed by peasants, who also grow rice. The process of harvesting the rice is mechanised, but the first crop of tea is harvested manually. The leaves are steamed, rolled and dried to stop fermentation, and the tea must be used quickly. These teas are stimulants and rich in vitamin C.

WHOLE LEAVES

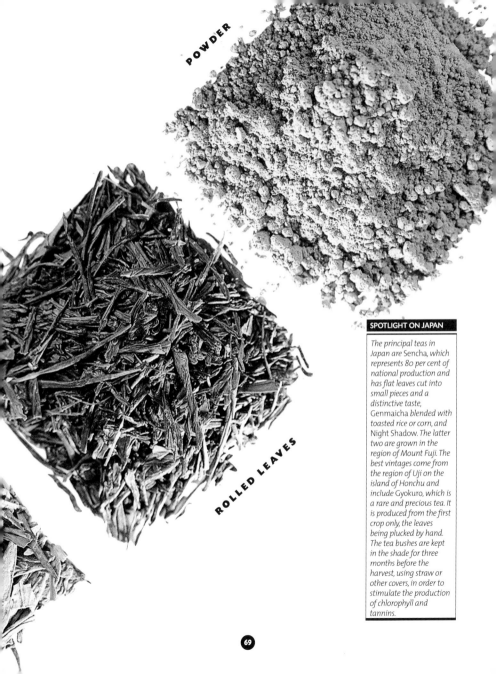

POWDER

ROLLED LEAVES

SPOTLIGHT ON JAPAN

The principal teas in Japan are Sencha, which represents 80 per cent of national production and has flat leaves cut into small pieces and a distinctive taste, Genmaicha blended with toasted rice or corn, and Night Shadow. The latter two are grown in the region of Mount Fuji. The best vintages come from the region of Uji on the island of Honchu and include Gyokuro, which is a rare and precious tea. It is produced from the first crop only, the leaves being plucked by hand. The tea bushes are kept in the shade for three months before the harvest, using straw or other covers, in order to stimulate the production of chlorophyll and tannins.

Blended, scented or smoked?

With their delicate flowery perfumes, subtle flavours of fruits and spices and deliciously exotic aromas, scented teas transport you instantly to the East.

Scented teas

Jasmine tea hails mainly from the province of Fujian, where it has been manufactured for centuries. It is made from green tea, which is first dried and then placed next to freshly gathered jasmine flowers and left for the evening. The developing aroma of the flowers scents the tea naturally. Sometimes the flowers are mixed in with the tea. It is not the quantity of flowers that matters but their quality and freshness. Although this is the method for making scented tea that has been handed down by Chinese tea-makers over the centuries, other methods are prevalent today. Most teas on the market are combined either with essences to give them a scent of flowers or with essential oils or alcohol-based flavours for the tang of citrus fruits.

Smoked tea

Low in caffeine and with a strong scent, smoked tea is made from Souchong leaves that are pan-fried in a wok, rolled, fermented, and then dried over a fire of spruce or cypress roots. The Chinese reserve this tea for export.

Blends of tea

The blends are made from tea that comes from different estates within the same region, and has been plucked at different times. It is a reliable way of maintaining the taste, regulating production and marketing large quantities. The most prized blends include English Breakfast and Afternoon Tea.

Earl Grey

Adapted from an old Chinese recipe, the production of *Earl Grey* tea can be traced back to the beginning of the 20th century. It is scented with oil of bergamot, a citrus fruit that is a hybrid of the lemon and the bigarade trees. *Earl Grey* teas from the province of Yunnan are some of the finest, while others are blends of tea of different origins: from China, Assam, Oolong from Taiwan, etc.

Bouquets, stars, buds and pearls – tea is as pleasing to the eye as it is to the palate.

It takes 100 kg (220 lb) of lotus flowers to scent just 1 kg (2.2 lb) of tea!

VANILLA

GINGER

ORANGE BLOSSOM

CINNAMON

LOTUS

MINT

JASMINE

RASPBERRY

COCONUT

The tea-producing countries

While the majority of teas sold are blends of different teas, specialist shops nonetheless offer 'single-estate' (or 'vintage') teas to satisfy an increasingly demanding clientele. These teas are sold under the name of their estate of origin to guarantee their source. Each national producer has its vintage teas, the most renowned coming from China, India, Sri Lanka (Ceylon) and Japan.

India

Offering endless varieties, India has now become the leading producer of tea, overtaking China. The main producing regions are Darjeeling, Assam, Dooars, Terai, Kangra, Cachar, Travancore, Nilgri and Sikkim. In Assam alone, one of the wildest areas in the country, there are more than 1,900 estates, accounting for 47 per cent of India's tea production.

Sri Lanka

The regions yielding the best vintages are those of Uva, Nuwaraeliya, Dimbulas, Ratnapura and Galle.
The larger estates of Uva produce some excellent vintages: for example *Uva Highlands* (all grades), *Saint James* (OP and Fannings), *Aislaby* (FP and *Fannings*), *Attempettia* (BOP), *Dyraaba* (BOP), *Roehampton*(BOP).

China

Apart from a tiny proportion of its production, China's great teas do not come from single estates. The production of different plantations that come under the same region are blended to produce teas with consistent characteristics which are defined according to a numbering system. Cultivated in 19 provinces and more than 900 regions, China's tiny plantations are grouped into state cooperatives producing black teas, green teas, semi-fermented teas and smoked teas.

Cultivated terraces in southern China.

World tea production
Amounts are expressed in tonnes

from 0 to 50,000

from 50,000 to 100,000

from 100,000 to 500,00

The great tea estates

From the gardens of Darjeeling to the vast plantations of Sri Lanka (where Ceylon tea is produced) tea has conquered a vast territory.

Darjeeling – the Champagne of Tea

The plantations are situated on the south-facing slopes of the mountain, at altitudes of 1,000–2134 metres (3,280–7,000 feet), where the average temperature varies from 8–25°C. The hot and humid climate of the monsoon season provides the ideal conditions for the tea plant.

Darjeeling tea is considered by some to be the 'champagne' of tea, even though it only constitutes 2 per cent of national production. A Tibetan name meaning 'place of thunderbolts', Darjeeling covers the region at the foot of the Himalayas and is the capital of Bengal.

Teas sold under the generic name of Darjeeling are blends of leaves from different estates, but the ones that bear the name of their estate of origin, some of which are sold for astronomical prices, are the most prized.

The teas of Ceylon

The British first tried to grow tea in Ceylon (now Sri Lanka) in the mid-19th century, but it wasn't until 1860 that a 26-year-old Scotsman, James Taylor, began tea production in earnest. Other farmers were quick to follow, including Thomas Lipton, who began buying old coffee plantations in 1890 at low prices after the crops had been devastated by rust.

Ceylon tea is divided into three categories according to the altitude of the plantations, which rise in terraces from sea level to a height of 2,500 metres (8,200 feet) and are located predominantly in the south. They are: low grown(LG), found below 600 metres (2,000 feet) – of average quality; mid-grown (MG), found at 600–1,200 metres (2,000–3,900 feet) – of very good quality; high grown (HG), found above 1,200 metres (3,900 feet) – of excellent quality.

THE 87 'GARDENS' OF DARJEELING

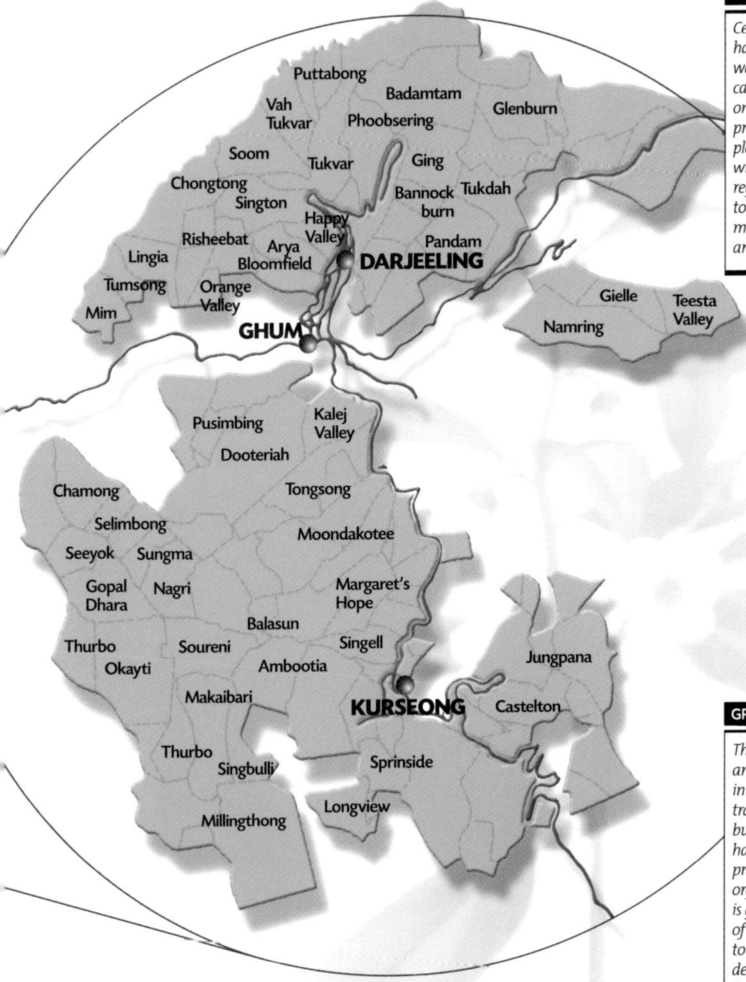
Puttabong
Badamtam
Vah
Tukvar
Glenburn
Phoobsering
Soom
Tukvar
Ging
Chongtong
Sington
Bannock burn
Tukdah
Happy Valley
Risheebat
Arya
Pandam
Lingia
Bloomfield
DARJEELING
Tumsong
Orange Valley
Gielle
Teesta Valley
Mim
GHUM
Namring
Pusimbing
Kalej Valley
Dooteriah
Chamong
Tongsong
Selimbong
Moondakotee
Seeyok
Sungma
Gopal Dhara
Nagri
Margaret's Hope
Balasun
Singell
Thurbo
Soureni
Jungpana
Okayti
Ambootia
Makaibari
KURSEONG
Castelton
Thurbo
Singbulli
Sprinside
Longview
Millingthong

CULTIVATION IN CEYLON

Ceylon tea is gathered by hand in the traditional way by women who carry the crop in baskets on their backs, as is the practice in India. Tea plants are kept in their wild state, but are set at regular distances in order to provide shade and make picking less arduous.

GREEN TEA IN INDIA

The processes of plucking and processing black tea in India are still based on traditional techniques, but more recently there has been a move towards producing high-quality organic green tea, which is grown without the use of pesticides or fertiliser, to meet Western demand. The most famous estates are Castelton, Jungpana, Margaret's Hope, Namring, Lingia, Seeyok, Risheehat and Bannockburn.

Russian tea

Tea in Russia is a black tea, often made in a samovar that heats the water and maintains its temperature.

A concentrated tea

Tea first appeared in the Russian empire towards the middle of the 17th century, and was originally drunk predominantly in the towns and cities, particularly Moscow. It became much more popular in the 19th century. Russian tea, which is highly concentrated, is poured into a cup and then hot water is added. It is drunk either with a lump of sugar in the mouth, or with honey or jam.

IMPRESSIONS OF RUSSIA

At dusk the samovar is gleaming

Upon the table, piping hot;

And as it hisses, gently steaming,

The vapour wreathes the china pot.

Now Olga sits before it, filling

The lustrous tea-cups, never spilling

A drop of the dark fragrant stream;

A serving-lad hands round the cream.

Apart, Tatyana can but linger

Beside the window; on the pane

She breathes again and yet again,

And in the mist her little finger

Describes in pensive tracery

The hallowed letters O and E.

A. Pushkin, *Eugene Onegin*,
translated from the Russian
by Babette Deutsch.

The preparation of tea on the Mongolian Steppes.

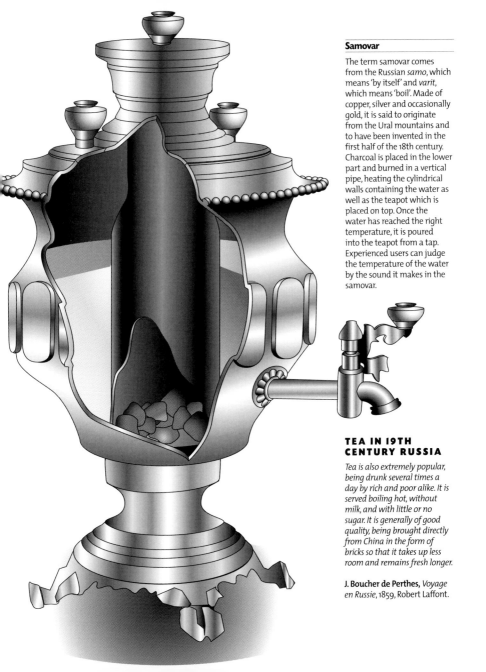

Samovar

The term samovar comes from the Russian *samo*, which means 'by itself' and *varit*, which means 'boil'. Made of copper, silver and occasionally gold, it is said to originate from the Ural mountains and to have been invented in the first half of the 18th century. Charcoal is placed in the lower part and burned in a vertical pipe, heating the cylindrical walls containing the water as well as the teapot which is placed on top. Once the water has reached the right temperature, it is poured into the teapot from a tap. Experienced users can judge the temperature of the water by the sound it makes in the samovar.

TEA IN 19TH CENTURY RUSSIA

Tea is also extremely popular, being drunk several times a day by rich and poor alike. It is served boiling hot, without milk, and with little or no sugar. It is generally of good quality, being brought directly from China in the form of bricks so that it takes up less room and remains fresh longer.

J. Boucher de Perthes, *Voyage en Russie,* 1859, Robert Laffont.

Tea in the East

Offering tea is an act of kindness that shows strangers that they are welcome.

The countries of North Africa

After the Crimean War in the 19th century, the British, having lost their Slav market, focused their commercial efforts on the countries of North Africa to clear their stocks of green tea. The tea-drinking habit was rapidly adopted and the Maghrebi peoples of the region invented a highly spiritual tea ceremony similar to the Japanese one, as the recipe was considered a 'gift from Allah'.

The Russians do not have a monopoly on the samovar – the Iranians, the Turks and the Maghrebi have their own version.

Tibet

The first imports of tea into Tibet date back to the 7th century AD when it arrived from the Chinese provinces of Yunnan and Sichuan on the backs of yaks. It was a long and arduous journey, and to ensure that the tea was properly preserved en route, it was transported in bricks. The Tibetans drink tea supplied in bricks to this day.

Tibetan tea

The brick of tea is crushed in a mortar, boiled in water, and then whisked together with yak's butter and some salt. The Tibetans sometimes add ginger, orange peel, spices, milk, or even onion and usually serve it in a wooden bowl. A prayer of offering is said before drinking. Tea is also the base ingredient of a traditional dish made with roasted barley flour and sometimes a little butter. The Mongols and the Nepalese also drink tea in a similar way, with minor variations.

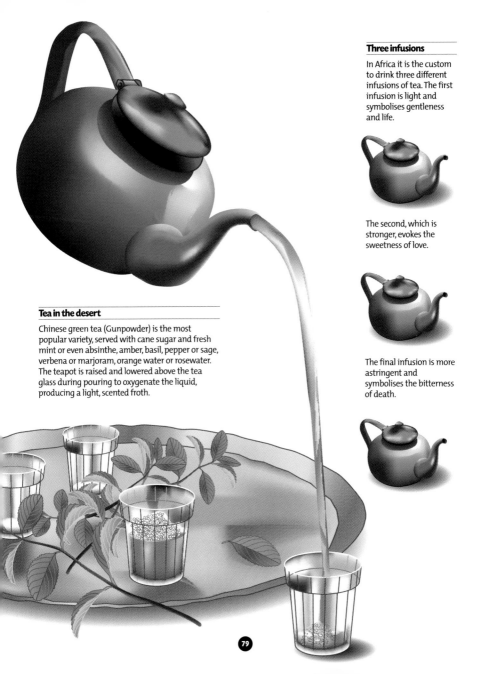

Three infusions

In Africa it is the custom to drink three different infusions of tea. The first infusion is light and symbolises gentleness and life.

The second, which is stronger, evokes the sweetness of love.

The final infusion is more astringent and symbolises the bitterness of death.

Tea in the desert

Chinese green tea (Gunpowder) is the most popular variety, served with cane sugar and fresh mint or even absinthe, amber, basil, pepper or sage, verbena or marjoram, orange water or rosewater. The teapot is raised and lowered above the tea glass during pouring to oxygenate the liquid, producing a light, scented froth.

Utensils

The three utensils used in the tea ceremony are the bamboo spoon ((chasaku), the bamboo whisk (chasen) and the tea bowl (chawan). The tea used is Matcha, a green tea that is whisked into a 'jade froth'.

The way to harmony

The guests kneel down side by side. The host arranges the charcoal in the brazier, then wipes the natsune (tea container) and the chasaku (bamboo spoon) with a silk cloth.

1 *The host takes some water from the kama (cast-iron kettle) using the hishaku (bamboo ladle) and pours it into the chawan (tea bowl).*

2 *The chasen (bamboo whisk) is rinsed in it, then the water is emptied and the chawan (tea bowl) is cleaned with a damp cloth.*

3 *Using the chasaku (bamboo spoon), the required amount of Matcha is taken from the natsune and placed in the chawan.*

4 *The host takes water from the kama using the hishaku and pours it into the chawan.*

5 *The liquid is whisked with the chasen.*

6 *The host pours more water from the kama.*

7 *The liquid is whisked with the chasen a second time.*

The guest of honour steps up to receive the bowl, returns to his place and takes three sips. In turn, the other guests drink from the same bowl. The guest of honour then returns the bowl to the host.

The tea ceremony should evoke four virtues: harmony, respect, purity and tranquillity.

The 'Chanoyu'

The *Chanoyu*, literally 'hot water for tea', follows a strict code, developed by the master Sen No Rikyû (1522–91). Great importance is placed on the setting in the tea house where the tea ceremony takes place. The guests pass through a symbolic door and then walk along some carefully laid flat stones to a garden designed to make them forget the outside world. In a second, or inner garden, the guests drink spring water directly from a wooden ladle and wash their hands to cleanse themselves. The host, dressed in a kimono, presides over the ceremony.

The quest for perfection

The tea ceremony is so elaborate that it is not possible to describe every single gesture here. There are two forms of ceremony – a simplified one called *chaikai* and the traditional one called *chaji*, which can last up to four hours. The latter involves three to five people and contains several hundred precise gestures relating to how the tea is prepared, from the use of the utensils to the movements of the host of the ceremony and the attitude of the guest of honour.

The seven golden rules

The tea ceremony must follow the seven rules taught by Sen No Rikyû: make a delicious bowl of tea, arrange the charcoal so that it heats the water, arrange the flowers as they are in the field, evoke coolness in summer and warmth in winter, do everything ahead of time, be prepared for rain, and pay the utmost attention to each of your guests.

A philosophy

The tea ceremony is an expression of a whole philosophy, which focuses on emptying the mind in order to contact the inner self, becoming detached from the material world by concentrating on the strict rules of the ceremony.

In good company

The Japanese have a delightful way of describing the act of making tea according to the number of people taking part. If tea is taken alone, it is drunk 'with contemplation'. If there are two people, it becomes an 'act of communion'. If there are three, it is drunk 'in a charming manner'. If more than three take tea, it is considered 'communal', unless it is to gather one's thoughts, in which case it is referred to as 'drinking in the open'.

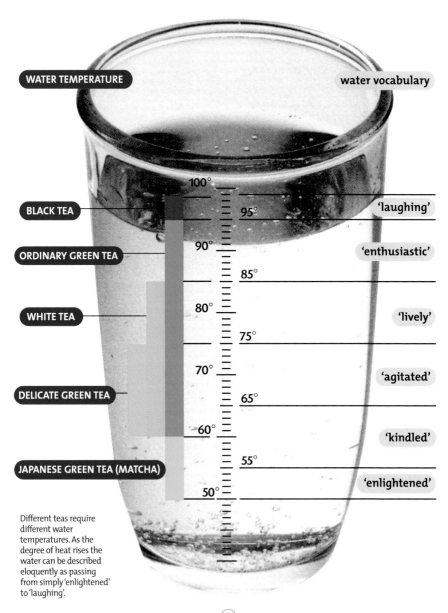

WATER TEMPERATURE

water vocabulary

BLACK TEA

ORDINARY GREEN TEA

WHITE TEA

DELICATE GREEN TEA

JAPANESE GREEN TEA (MATCHA)

100°
95° — 'laughing'
90°
85° — 'enthusiastic'
80°
75° — 'lively'
70°
65° — 'agitated'
60°
55° — 'kindled'
50° — 'enlightened'

Different teas require
different water
temperatures. As the
degree of heat rises the
water can be described
eloquently as passing
from simply 'enlightened'
to 'laughing'.

The importance of water

Storing tea

Tea absorbs odours from the atmosphere and is sensitive to humidity, temperature and light. For this reason, the kitchen is not necessarily the best place to store it. Always use an opaque and watertight container such as a metal tin or a ceramic pot. Black tea can be kept for a long time, sometimes several years if stored according to the instructions, but it is probably better not to exceed one or two years. Green tea should be consumed within 6–12 months.

Tin of tea from Mariage Frères.

The preparation of tea follows certain rules that must be observed carefully to obtain a delicately scented infusion.

Quality of water

One day, an important dignitary asked the Chinese poet Lu Yu to taste some water that was highly regarded in a particular region. His verdict was: 'I would say that this water came from the main river of Namling, but it has been greatly diluted with water from the banks of the river.' And he was quite right. The story may be apocryphal, but it nonetheless shows that waters can taste different to a connoisseur. For tea, Lu Yu recommended using mountain water or, failing that, river water, and last but not least, spring water. Nowadays, the top choice would be slightly sparkling spring water from a superior source, followed by mineral water that has been pumped from a great depth and that contains large amounts of minerals, and lastly tap water, which may have been treated with chemicals.

Tap water

Tap water is rarely the best to use for tea-making because of the filtration systems and substances such as chlorine that are added to make it safe to drink.

Water temperature

The temperature of the water plays a vital role in the quality of tea. Boiling water will burn the tea, removing some of its flavours. Boiled water will be too chalky, too hard, and in particular, it will have lost its oxygen, which takes the life out of the liquid, making it flat and dull. Generally speaking, if the tea is delicate, the temperature of the water should not be too high.

The finer points of the perfect cup

While the tea itself should be chosen to suit the time of day, the quantity of tea is important for obtaining a good brew.

How to measure tea

Deciding how much tea to use is largely a matter of trial and error. The general guideline is one teaspoonful of tea per cup and one for the pot. Although this method is easy to put into practice, it is oversimplified, and it may be better to weigh the tea. One teaspoonful is about 2–2.5 g (0.07–0.09 oz) of tea but will weigh more if the tea is fanning and less if it is whole leaves.

Large tea leaves require longer brewing than broken leaves, which have a greater surface area in contact with the water.

Sugar, milk or lemon?

Tea is naturally bitter and can be an acquired taste, though sugar helps to mask this. In Afghanistan, Russia, Egypt, North Africa and even occasionally in India, tea is drunk with sugar in varying quantities, cane sugar being the best for retaining the flavour of the tea. The British, having learned to drink tea in the company of the Manchus, who were great milk drinkers, adopted the habit of adding milk to their tea. The main concern ever since has been whether to put the milk in the cup before or after pouring the tea (although most connoisseurs agree that the milk should be poured first). Some people prefer to add lemon to their tea to soften the strong flavour, however, lemon changes the colour and destroys the taste of the tea. A slice of orange would be better.

TEA IN BAGS?

In Europe 75 per cent of tea is consumed in tea bags. Unfortunately, this method of infusion doesn't allow the full quality of the contents to be appreciated. Some very good teas come in tea bags, but the vast majority of them, particularly those served in cafés, are of poor quality. The other disadvantage is that they kill the flavour – the taste of paper inhibits the subtleties of the drink and the tea is crushed inside most tea bags because there isn't enough room for the leaves to spread out. What's more, with tagged teabags, the string and paper are sometimes treated with chlorine and the aluminium staple adds a hint of acidity. Muslin tea bags are therefore a better choice.

Infusion time in minutes | Quantity in grams per 10 cl (3.5 fl oz)

15 10 5 0 5 15

japanese green tea

white tea

chinese green tea

oolong tea

black tea (whole leaves)

black tea (broken leaves)

black tea (fanning)

aromatic tea

Which teapot?

SILVER TEAPOT

CAST-IRON TEAPOT

PORCELAIN TEAPOT

CLAY TEAPOT

For some people, the pleasures of the palate and aesthetic ideals cannot be separated, so their choice of teapot depends on how elegant it looks, how fine the porcelain, and how attractive its design. Others are more interested in the practical features of a teapot.

A teapot for every tea

Teapots whose interior surfaces are glazed do not retain the flavour of tea, unlike those with porous surfaces such as unglazed clay or cast-iron, so if you have only one teapot, it's better to have one with a shiny inner surface, such as glazed clay, porcelain or glass, as it won't hold or mix the different flavours. Tea connoisseurs recommend one teapot for black teas from India (Assam or Darjeeling), Ceylon, and Africa, another for black teas from China, another for green teas from Japan, and yet another for scented teas (Jasmine, Earl Grey, and so on). In this case, you should select a teapot that retains the flavours, where a deposit forms on the inside surface, coating the teapot and 'seasoning' it. Some experts recommend Japanese clay teapots that have been glazed on the outside, while others prefer those made of cast iron.

Metal teapots

Teapots made of silver or metal are reserved for mint green teas but should not be used for delicate teas. The metal gives an acidic taste, which is excellent for counteracting the bitterness of mint tea, but destroys all other flavours. When a teapot is brand new, you should prepare it by warming it a few times, then brewing several pots of tea in it.

Did you know?

A teapot should only be used for tea. Herbal infusions such as verbena, for instance, would give the teapot a taste that would kill the flavours of tea.

Tea time

Tea time has long been used to refer to the hour at which tea is taken. However, as more varieties of tea become available and social drinking, whether among workers on a building site or ladies with their friends, becomes increasingly popular, tea time now can be almost any time of day.

Cup, mug, bowl or zhong?

Tea lovers believe in serving tea in the right receptacle and can become quite obsessive about their favourite cup. Cup, mug or bowl – the choice is yours.

Cup, mug or bowl

Always choose a receptacle with a white background so that you can appreciate the colour of the liquid, and don't fill it to the top or the flavours won't develop properly. Vintage Chinese teas and the Japanese Gyokuro are drunk in tiny sips from cups the size of a thimble. During the tea ceremony in Japan, green tea is drunk by several people from the same bowl.

... or zhong ?

The Chinese use a *zhong* (or *chung*), which is a cup with a lid and a deep saucer but no handle. It replaces the teapot, which is considered unsuitable for preparing green tea. It is used for drinking as well as infusing.

Tea strainers

Although some cast-iron teapots and, more recently, porcelain and glass ones come equipped with a filter designed to hold the tea leaves, in most cases tea still needs straining. Metal equipment, such as mesh tea balls, tong infusers and tea strainers should be avoided as they can affect the taste. What's more, tea balls and tongs squash the tea and can prevent the leaves from releasing their flavours. The best solution is the cloth sock, which is available in different sizes to suit the teapot, a nylon strainer or the cotton filter which allows you to stop the infusion at the right moment.

How to prepare tea in a zhong

Place green tea in the *zhong* and add water heated to 70°C, then drain it away immediately. This hydrates and rinses the leaves. Repeat the process, this time allowing it to brew for two to four minutes, leaving the lid on to retain the flavours. Finally, taste the tea. The Chinese brew their tea two or three times.

TEA BALL

TEA TONGS AND STRAINER

TEA GLASS　　　　**TEA CUP**　　　　**MUG**

TEA BOWL

The benefits of tea

At the time of plucking, a tea leaf is 75–85 per cent water. Its dry substances comprise 20–35 per cent tannins, 20–30 per cent protein (of which only albumin is soluble in water), 20–25 per cent carbohydrates (not very soluble in water), 4–5 per cent fat (not very soluble in water), 3–5 per cent organic acids, 3–5 per cent caffeine, and more than 500 aromatic substances. It is also rich in amino acids, vitamins (A, B, C, E and P), minerals such as potassium, magnesium, calcium, sodium (in minute quantities in brewed tea, which makes it permissible in salt-free diets), phosphorous, manganese, copper, iron and fluoride (in great quantities, particularly in green tea).

The benefits attributed to tea in recent years have helped boost its popularity throughout Europe.

Beneficial qualities

The caffeine contained in tea (also called theine) is less harmful than that found in coffee and produces different effects. It gently stimulates the nervous system improving concentration for an appreciable period. It may have a positive effect on the cardiovascular and respiratory systems as well as on arteriosclerosis and is also considered to be beneficial for the three levels of cholesterol (very low, low, and high density lipoproteins).

Numerous other elements in tea can also help regulate the body's processes and it is often used in Chinese herbal medicines. However, it is important to remember that Chinese medicine is preventative; it may not heal, but it can help protect against certain diseases.

Tea also helps fight the ageing process by acting on the free radicals. But it can do much more: it is anti-viral (psoriasis, shingles), anti-bacterial (staphylococcus, dysentery, typhoid fever), it inhibits the clumping of platelets in the blood and prevents thrombosis and cerebral haemorrhage. It also fights against heart failure, arrythmia, diabetes, asthma, stomach ulcers, constipation, ophthalmic disorders, tooth decay and much more.

Green tea plays a diuretic role, particularly in Chinese herbal medicine, in that it helps eliminate water and toxins. It contains flavonoids and can be used as part of a planned diet to arrest the assimilation of carbohydrates and fats.

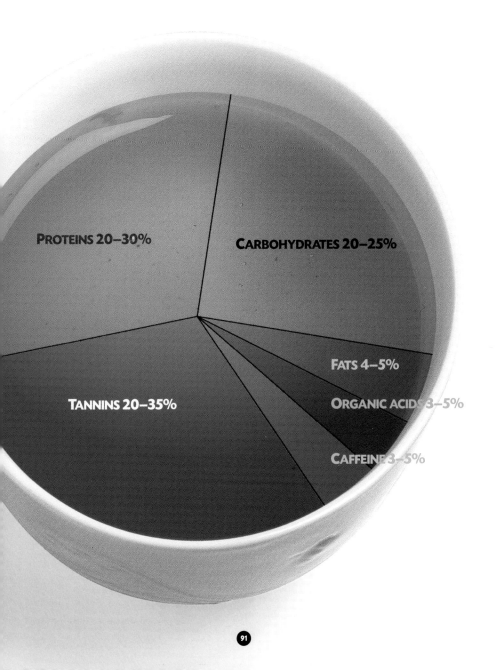

PROTEINS 20–30%

CARBOHYDRATES 20–25%

FATS 4–5%

TANNINS 20–35%

ORGANIC ACIDS 3–5%

CAFFEINE 3–5%

Matcha-topped sea bream fillets with a warm vinaigrette

 1. Fillet and scale the fish, keeping the trimmings to make a stock.

2. To make the stock, crush the trimmings and peel and finely chop the carrot and onion. Tie together the parsley, thyme and bay leaf. Place the trimmings, carrots, onions and herbs in a large casserole, add a pinch of salt and the juice of half a lemon, cover with a litre (1.8 pints) of water and boil for 20 minutes. Remove the herbs and pass stock through a fine sieve and reserve.

3. Mix the sea salt with two teaspoons of *Matcha* tea and spread a thin layer of this mixture onto each scaled fillet. Press down with your hands and put to one side.

4. Peel the turnips and slice very thinly. Pour the sunflower oil into a deep frying pan.

5. To prepare the warm vinaigrette, mix the two oils, soy sauce, balsamic vinegar and two spoonfuls of stock in a saucepan. Heat gently, whisking the ingredients at the same time. Add the rest of the green tea. Whisk and keep warm in a double boiler.

6. Light the grill. Heat the oil in the frying pan.

7. Grill the bream fillets gently and while they are cooking prepare the turnip slices. When the oil in the pan is hot, place them in the frying pan and fry until they start to turn golden. Remove them from the pan with a slotted spoon and place on some absorbent kitchen paper.

8. Place each Matcha-coated fillet on a separate plate, add the turnip slices and warm vinaigrette and serve immediately.

HOW LONG DOES IT TAKE?

Preparation time: 15 mins
Cooking time: 8 mins

SERVES 4

4 fillets of sea bream (or sea bass), each weighing about 200 g (7 oz)
3 heaped teaspoons of Matcha or other green tea
4 teaspoons of sea salt
4 good-quality turnips
250 ml (9 fl oz) sunflower oil
2 tablespoons grapeseed oil
1 tablespoon fruity olive oil
1 tablespoon soy sauce
1 tablespoon balsamic vinegar

FOR THE STOCK

1 carrot
1 onion
1 bay leaf
1 sprig of thyme
A few stems of parsley
Half a lemon

Veal aiguillettes in orange tea sauce

1. Peel the large carrot and celeriac and cut into fine sticks. Blanch the tomato, remove the skin and seeds and cut into small cubes. Cook the baby carrots in boiling, salted water for a few minutes
and cool them with ice cubes so that they retain their crunchiness. Place to one side.

2. Squeeze the oranges and reduce the juice over a low heat with the honey and the diced tomato. Prepare the veal stock.

3. Thinly slice the shallots and the mushrooms and fry them gently in 20 g (3/4oz) butter. Pour in the white wine and cook for two to three minutes. Add the veal stock and the slightly concentrated orange juice, season to taste and simmer until reduced.

4. Brew the tea for four minutes in the reduced liquid. Add the crème fraîche, pass through a strainer and adjust the seasoning if necessary. Keep warm in a double boiler.

5. Sweat the carrot and celeriac sticks in 20 g (3/4oz) butter, adding salt and pepper and a little water, cover and allow to simmer for five minutes. Add the baby carrots at the end of the cooking time to heat them through.

6. Place 10 g (1/2oz) butter in a non-stick pan, and fry the veal steaks over a high heat for four minutes on each side to seal them. Place the vegetables on warm plates, add the sliced steaks and the baby carrots and pour over the tea sauce.

HOW LONG DOES IT TAKE?

Preparation and cooking time: approx. 1 hour 15 mins

SERVES 4

4 thick-cut veal steaks, about 1 1/2 cm (1/2 in) thick
1 bunch of baby carrots
300 g (10 oz) large carrots
300 g (10 oz) celeriac
1 ripe tomato
Juice of 4 oranges
1 tablespoon honey
200 ml (7 fl oz) veal stock (instant)
4 shallots
100 g (3 1/2 oz) mushrooms
50 g (2 oz) butter
100 ml (3 1/2 fl oz) sweet white wine
Sea salt
Freshly milled pepper
10 g (1/2oz) tea(s) scented with orange and vanilla
100 ml (3 1/2 fl oz) crème fraîche

Mango tart with Vanilla ice-cream

Vanilla tea ice-cream

HOW LONG DOES IT TAKE?

Preparation time: 10 mins
Cooking time: 15 mins
Cooling time: approx. 25 mins

SERVES 4

30 g (1 1/2 oz) vanilla tea
1 litre (1 3/4 pints) full-fat, pasteurised milk
4 egg yolks
100 g (3 1/2 oz) caster sugar
125g (4 oz) single cream

1. First prepare the ice-cream. Boil the milk and pour over the tea, allowing to infuse for two minutes before passing through a strainer.

2. Beat the egg yolks with the sugar until pale and add the milk scented with the vanilla tea.

3. Return to a low heat and cook the mixture, stirring all the time until it thickens and coats the spoon. Pour immediately into a large bowl through a strainer, add the single cream and leave to cool before placing in an ice-cream maker.

4. Roll out the flaky pastry and cut out four circles, 15cm (6 in) in diameter. Preheat the oven to 200°C (Gas mark 6).

5. Peel and thinly slice the mango and arrange the slices in a rose pattern on the pastry. Top with a few knobs of butter, brown sugar and sprinkle with a small pinch of the vanilla tea. Place in the oven and cook for 15 minutes until the pastry turns golden.

6. While the tarts are still warm and crisp, place a scoop of ice-cream on top of each tart and serve.

Mango tart

HOW LONG DOES IT TAKE?

Preparation time: 10 mins
Cooking time: 15 mins

MAKES 4 TARTLETS

250 g (9 oz) ready-made flaky pastry
1 large mango
80 g (3 oz) butter
50 g (2 oz) brown sugar
10 g (1/2 oz) vanilla tea

Green tea macaroons

 1. First prepare the butter cream.

2. Boil the sugar and the water for about five minutes until small bubbles form on the surface.

3. Whisk the egg yolks.

4. Trickle the boiling syrup into the egg yolks, while continuing to whisk vigorously for three minutes, then stir gently until the mixture cools.

5. Incorporate the butter a bit at a time, add the powdered green tea and whisk for five minutes until the ingredients are evenly mixed. Place to one side.

6. Preheat the oven to 200°C (gas mark 6). For fan-assisted ovens, preheat to 180°C (gas mark 4).

7. Mix together the ground almonds, icing sugar and vanilla sugar.

8. Sieve four times.

9. Beat the egg whites with a few drops of lemon and a little caster sugar until stiff.

10. Sprinkle the rest of the sugar on top.

11. Place a sheet of greaseproof paper, folded in two, on a baking tray.

12. Carefully fold the sieved ingredients into the beaten egg whites with a spatula.

13. Pour into a piping bag with a smooth nozzle 5 1/2 mm (1/4 in) in diameter.

14. Pipe circles of the mixture about 4 cm (1 1/2 in) in diameter onto the greaseproof paper, spaced evenly. Flatten with a wet brush.

15. Put in the oven and bake for 12 minutes.

16. When half the cooking time has elapsed, prop the oven door half-open with a wooden spoon.

17. When the macaroons are cooked, trickle some cold water between the greaseproof paper and the baking tray without wetting the macaroons. This will make them easier to remove.

18. When cool, sandwich the macaroons together by placing a good-sized knob of butter cream on one of the macaroons and another macaroon on top.

HOW LONG DOES IT TAKE?

Preparation time: 30 mins
Cooking time: 20 mins

MAKES 24 MACAROONS

625 g (1lb 6oz) ground almonds
125 g (4 oz) icing sugar
2 sachets of vanilla sugar
500 g (1lb 2oz) egg white
6 drops of lemon juice
125 g (4 oz) caster sugar

BUTTER CREAM

400 g (14 oz) sugar
330 ml (11 1/2 fl oz) water
7 egg yolks
500 g (1lb 2 oz) soft butter
4 teaspoons of powdered Matcha or other green tea

Crème brûlée with Butterscotch tea

 1. Bring the milk to the boil and pour it onto the tea. Allow to infuse for five minutes then pass through a strainer.

2. Beat the egg yolks and caster sugar in a bowl until the mixture turns pale, then add the milk scented with the Butterscotch tea.

3. Whisk everything together, incorporating the crème fraîche at the same time, until the ingredients are evenly mixed.

4. Divide the mixture between 4 ramekin dishes and bake in the oven at 150°C (gas mark 2) for 30 minutes.

5. Allow to cool and place in the refrigerator for one hour.

6. Sprinkle the crèmes with granulated sugar and place under the grill for one to two minutes until the tops caramelise.

7. Serve warm or cold.

HOW LONG DOES IT TAKE?

Preparation time: 20 mins
Cooking time: 35 mins
Standing time: 30 mins

SERVES 4

200 ml (7 1/2 fl oz) milk
2 teaspoons of Butterscotch tea scented with chocolate and caramel
250 g (7 1/2 oz) crème fraîche
4 egg yolks
100 g (3 1/2 oz) caster sugar
20 g (3/4 oz) granulated sugar

Scented tea cream desserts

 1. Bring the milk to the boil, then pour 250 ml (9 oz) into four bowls each containing a different tea. Allow to infuse for three minutes and strain each one separately.

2. Break the whole eggs into a bowl and add the egg yolks and the caster sugar. Mix without beating. Add the crème fraîche. Weigh the mixture and divide between the four bowls, blending it with the scented milk teas.

3. Heat the oven to 180°C (gas mark 4). Using a flame-proof gratin dish, fill with sufficient water to come half-way up the cream pots, then fill each pot with the mixture. Place in the oven for about 15 minutes. To check that they are done, move one of the pots gently. The cream should wobble.

4. Serve warm or cold.

HOW LONG DOES IT TAKE?

Preparation time: 15 mins
Cooking time: 15 mins

MAKES 8 CREAM DESSERTS

4 egg yolks
2 whole eggs
50 g (2 oz) caster sugar
1 litre (1 3/4 pints) full-fat pasteurised milk
250 g (9 oz) crème fraîche
3 teaspoons mint green tea
3 teaspoons Lapsang Souchong
3 teaspoons Jasmine tea
3 teaspoons Earl Grey tea

Mint tea

 1. Remove the leaves from two sprigs of mint.

2. Place the green tea in a teapot.

3. Add a small quantity of simmering water and then drain immediately.

4. Add the mint leaves and 500 ml (17 1/2 fl oz) simmering water.

5. Add the sugar, mix everything together and allow to infuse for six minutes.

6. Pour the tea into glasses through a strainer and garnish with a sprig of mint.

HOW LONG DOES IT TAKE?	MAKES 4 GLASSES
Preparation time: 10 mins	*6 sprigs of fresh mint* *2 teaspoons of Gunpowder or other green tea* *40 g (1 3/4 oz) caster sugar*

Spicy iced tea

 1. Bring 500 ml (17 1/2 fl oz) water to the boil.

2. Add the mixed spice, cinnamon, nutmeg, and ginger and then the tea.

3. Allow to simmer on a low heat for five minutes.

4. Remove from the heat, cover and allow to infuse for ten minutes.

5. Strain and leave to cool, then place in the refrigerator.

6. Divide equally into large glasses the orange and lemon juice, honey, some ice cubes, and then the tea.

7. Stir and serve.

HOW LONG DOES IT TAKE?	MAKES 4 GLASSES
Preparation time: 10 mins	*1 pinch mixed spice* *1 pinch cinnamon* *1 pinch nutmeg* *1 pinch ginger* *2 teaspoons of tea scented with citrus fruit* *2 tablespoons acacia honey* *200 ml (7 fl oz) orange juice* *Juice of half a lemon* *Ice cubes*

FIND OUT

WRITERS AND FILM DIRECTORS INSPIRED BY THE MEMORY OF A CUP OF TEA.
WHERE TO FIND THE BEST VINTAGE TEAS AND A SELECTION OF TEA ROOMS
TO VISIT. OTHER USES FOR TEA IN THE HOME. USEFUL ADDRESSES.

The grand master
Soshitsu Sen

Grand master of Japanese tea, and the fifteenth to bear this name, Soshitsu Sen steers over two million pupils through the traditions associated with tea in the school of Urasenke. Here, he describes the tea ceremony.

Curls of steam escape from the kettle. The sound of boiling water is like the sound of the wind blowing through pine trees.

The host puts powdered tea into the bowl, adds a little hot water, mixes them together with a whisk, adds a little more water, whisks the mixture again and offers it to the first guest. The air is serene and filled with the scent of tea. All the guests share this bowl of strong, dark green tea. They may ask to take a closer look at the tea container, the silk cloth and the teaspoon. While they do so, the host tidies away all the other utensils. He returns to the tea room to answer questions on the items that the guests have examined. Where was the tea container made? Who carved the spoon? Does it have a special name? When there are no more questions, the host gathers together the utensils and leaves the room, bowing to his guests from the door. He soon returns, bringing with him the utensils for serving light tea. The atmosphere is now more relaxed and the pace quickens. The host pours each guest a bowl of tea. They eat small cakes just before the host mixes the tea with the whisk. During this time, the guests can converse discreetly and ask to take a closer look at the new tea container and spoon. They ask about the lacquer, the shape of the container, the craft worker who made it and the name of the spoon. Afterwards, in silence, they admire the flowers and the fire once more.

The host opens the door to the corridor, bows to take his leave, and waits on the doorstep until all his guests have left.

He then sits for a moment to meditate on the meeting, clears away the utensils, washes them, removes the flower from the alcove and cleans the room again. The tea room is empty. To the untrained eye, it would appear that nothing extraordinary has taken place, but to the host and his guests, this experience is nothing short of a microcosm of life itself.

Soshitsu Sen, *Le Zen et le thé*, Editions SELD/Jean-Cyrille Godefroy, 1987.

Through the eyes of the West

Portuguese essayist Wenceslau de Morães devoted his life and works to the country of Japan where he spent more than 30 years. He is the author of *Culte du thé* (1905) and in 1897 published Dai-Nippon, O Grande Japão in which he presents a Westerner's view of the everyday method of drinking tea in Japan.

It's a drink for one and all, for rich and poor, a drink that quenches the thirst and fills the palace with subtle fragrances. Its slightly intoxicating, heady quality may be what gives these good people their cheerful manner, light sleep, acuteness of feeling, and a hint of perpetual, infectious excitement, which can be discerned in those shining black eyes, their mockery, and their roars of laughter.

My dearest wish for this country, Japan, which I love to the very depth of my being, is that it never ceases to drink tea! Tea, with all the paraphernalia required to make it, the little pewter tin, the portable stove, the cast-iron kettle, the tiny teapot, the five small porcelain cups and the five engraved metal saucers; tea, which is offered to a visitor upon the first greeting, as a sign of hospitality, of the pleasure of meeting and of fraternal communion; tea is the constant companion of the worker and the artist in their daily tasks, of the mousmé in her whims, and of all intimate gatherings; one could say it is the symbol of the family within the tender tranquillity of the nest.

Wenceslau de Morães, excerpt from *Dai-Nippon, O Grande Japão,* in *Le Culte du thé,* Editions La Différence, 1998.

The French art of tea

In the following excerpt from his book, *Swann's Way*, Marcel Proust suggests that partaking of an excellent cup of tea has been elevated to an art form in France.

But he never went to her house. Twice only, in the day-time, had he done so, to take part in the ceremony – of such vital importance in her life – of 'afternoon tea'.

She poured out Swann's tea, inquired 'Lemon or cream?' and, on his answering 'Cream, please,' said to him with a laugh: 'A cloud!' And as he pronounced it excellent, 'You see, I know just how you like it.' This tea had indeed seemed to Swann, just as it seemed to her, something precious, and love has such a need to find some justification for itself, some guarantee of duration, in pleasures which without it would have no existence and must cease with its passing, that when he left her at seven o'clock to go and dress for the evening, all the way home in his brougham, unable to repress the happiness with which the afternoon's adventure had filled him, he kept repeating to himself: 'How nice it would be to have a little woman like that in whose house one could always be certain of finding, what one never can be certain of finding, a really good cup of tea.'

Marcel Proust,, *Du côté de chez Swann*, Editions Gallimard, 1954; Translation from *Swann's Way*, Chatto & Windus and Random House, Inc. 1981.

A little Irish air

In the opening pages of *Ulysses* by James Joyce, which was published in 1922, two university friends meet for a traditional Irish breakfast – washed down with strong, sweet, black tea.

The blessings of God on you, Buck Mulligan cried, jumping up from his chair. Sit down. Pour out the tea there. The sugar is in the bag. Here, I can't go fumbling at the damned eggs. He hacked through the fry on the dish and slapped it out on three plates, saying:

In nominee Patris et Filii et Spiritus Sancti.

Haines sat down to pour out the tea.

- I'm giving you two lumps each, he said. But, I say, Mulligan, you do make strong tea, don't you?

Buck Mulligan, hewing thick slices from the loaf, said in an old woman's wheedling voice:

- When I makes tea I makes tea, as old mother Grogan said. And when I makes water I makes water.

- By Jove, it is tea, Haines said.

Buck Mulligan went on hewing and wheedling:

So I do, Mrs Cahill, says she. *Begob, ma'am* says Mrs Cahill, God send you don't make them in the one pot.

James Joyce, *Ulysses*, Penguin Books, 1992.

Tea aids the detecting powers of Lord Peter Wimsey

In her classic work of detective fiction Dorothy L. Sayers provides a strong pot of tea, some buttered tea-cakes and a willing listener to help Lord Peter Wimsey begin to solve the mystery of Philip Boyes' death.

'Well, now', said Wimsey, 'why do people kill people ?' ...

Miss Climpson poured out a cup of tea before replying. She wore a quantity of little bangles on her spare, lace-covered wrists, and they clinked aggressively with every movement.

'I really don't know,' she said, apparently taking the problem as a psychological one, 'it is so dangerous, as well as so terribly wicked, one wonders that anybody has the effrontery to undertake it. And very often they gain so little by it.'

'That's what I mean,' said Wimsey, 'what do they set out to gain ? Of course, some people seem to do it for the fun of the thing, like that German female, what's her name, who enjoyed seeing people die.'

'Such a strange taste,' said Miss Climpson. 'No sugar, I think ?' ...

'There is - passion,' said Miss Climpson, with a slight initial hesitation at the word, 'for I should not like to call it love, when it is so unregulated.'

'That is the explanation put forward by the prosecution,' said Wimsey. 'I don't accept it.'

'Certainly not. But - it might be possible, might it not, that there was some other unfortunate young woman who was attached to this Mr Boyes, and felt vindictively towards him ?'

'Yes, or a man who was jealous. But the time is the difficulty. You've got to have some plausible pretext for giving a bloke arsenic. You can't just catch him standing on a doorstep, and say, "Here, have a drink of this," can you ?'

Miss Climpson agreed, and buttered a second tea-cake.

'Then, insurance. Now we come to the region of the possible. Was Boyes insured ? It doesn't seem to have occurred to anybody to find out. Probably he wasn't. Literary blokes have very little forethought, and are careless about trifles like premiums. But one ought to know. Who might have an insurable interest? His father, his cousin (possibly), other relations (if any), his children (if any) and – I suppose – Miss Vane, if he took out the policy while he was living with her. Also anybody who may have lent him money on the strength of such insurance. Plenty of possibilities there. I'm feeling better already, Miss Climpson, fitter and brighter in every way. Either I'm getting a line on the thing, or else it's your tea. That's a good, stout-looking pot. Has it got any more in it ?'

'Yes, indeed,' said Miss Climpson, eagerly. 'My dear father used to say I was a great hand at getting the utmost out of a tea-pot. The secret is to fill up as you go and never empty the pot completely.'

Dorothy L. Sayers,
Strong Poison
Victor Gollancz, 1930.

A selection of teas

Listed below is a selection of teas on the market from all over the world, from the rarest to the most popular, the unusual to the classic. These form a substantial introduction to the world of tea.

CHINA

WHITE TEAS
These teas are characterised by their rarity. They are refreshing, but an acquired taste.

Bai Mu Dan (or *Pai Mu Tan*), province of Fujian, the perfect introduction to white tea, a great afternoon tea.

Yin Zhen, province north of *Fujian* and *Hunan*, a prestigious tea with a subtle aroma.

GREEN TEAS
Green teas from China are some of the best in the world. They develop very delicate flavours and their taste is highly valued.

Bi Luo Chun (or *Pi Lo Chun*), province of Jiangsu, rare, a great midday tea.

Ding Gu Da Fang, province of *Anhui*, an afternoon tea, ideal for the more experienced palette.

Gunpowder, the most common green tea, also used to make mint tea, can be drunk at any time of day.

Huang Shan Mao Feng (or *Hangshan Mao Feng*), province of Anhui.

Long Jing (or *Lung Ching*), province of *Zhejiang* (beware of imitations).

Sencha, tea with lots of flavour, the perfect accompaniment to meals.

Tai Ping Hou Kui (or *Taiping Houkui*), province of Anhui.

SEMI-FERMENTED OR OOLONG TEAS
The Chinese find **Oolong** teas extremely beneficial for the health and export very few of them.

Feng Huang Dan Cong (or *Fenghuang Dancong*), rare tea from the province of Guangdong, evening tea (beware of imitations).

Shui Hsien, province of Fujian and Guangdong, a mild, daytime tea.

Ti Kuan Yin, province of Fujian, the best known Chinese semi-fermented tea with delicate flavours.

BLACK TEAS
Some top vintages and some teas generally quite low in caffeine.

Jiangxi imperial, TGFOP1*, province of Jiangxi, the finest Chinese black tea, for afternoon drinking. *Experts add a '1' after the designation to signify first-class quality.

Keemun, FOP, province of Anhui, an afternoon or evening tea.

Pu Er (or *Pu Erh*), province of *Yunnan*, a beneficial tea with medicinal properties.

Sichuan, FOP, province of *Sichuan*, an afternoon tea.

Yunnan imperial, TGFOP, province of Yunnan, a top-quality tea, taken with breakfast.

SMOKED BLACK TEAS
Predominantly produced in the province of Fujian, most of these teas are reserved for export.

Lapsang Souchong, province of Fujian, moderately smoked.

Tarry Souchong, province of Fujian, highly smoked.

Yu Pao, province of Fujian, lightly smoked.

FORMOSA (Taiwan)

GREEN TEAS
Less renowned than the Chinese green teas, they are also cheaper.

Gunpowder Zhu Cha, a very refreshing tea used to make mint tea.

Pi Lo Chun, tea to be enjoyed in the late afternoon.

SEMI-FERMENTED OR OOLONG TEAS
These are the teas that made Formosa's reputation. They are drunk without milk or sugar.

Dong Ding Wu Long (or *Tung Ting*), moderately fermented (40 per cent), one of the island's best teas.

Fancy Oolong, a highly fermented tea (60–70 per cent), for late afternoon or evening.

Pouchong, a slightly fermented (10 per cent) daytime tea.

SMOKED BLACK TEAS
English breakfast or brunch teas.

INDIA

ASSAM BLACK TEAS
High-quality teas with a strong taste.

The first flush teas are rarely sold in Europe.

Bamonpookri, TGFOP, first flush, a breakfast tea.

Betjan, GFBOP, second flush, a full-flavoured breakfast tea.

Meleng, FOP, second flush, full-flavoured tea suitable for breakfast.

Napuk, FTGFOP1, second flush, a morning tea.

Nonaipara, TGFOP, first flush, daytime tea.

Silonibari, TGFOP, famous estate, a good accompaniment to savoury dishes.

Tara, FOP, second flush, an afternoon tea.

GREEN TEAS
Produced on a small scale but still worth investigating.

Khongea, the perfect tea for a relaxing break.

DARJEELING BLACK TEAS
A wide range of delicate teas. The first flush are light and scented, the second flush more fruity and full flavoured, and the in between combine youth and maturity.

Badamtam, FTGFOP1, second flush, excellent tea for any time of day.

Bloomfield, GFOP, first flush, very large estate, an afternoon tea.

Castelton, SFTGFOP1, second flush, vintage, the most valued of Indian teas.

Gielle, FTGFOP, second flush, a fine tea for any time of day.

Makaibari, FTGFOP1, first flush, an excellent afternoon tea.

Margaret's Hope, SFTGFOP1, first flush, a top-quality scented tea for connoisseurs.

Margaret's Hope, TGBOP1, second flush, a morning tea.

Namring, TGBOP, first flush, for those who like a dash of milk in their tea.

Namring Upper, SFTGFOP1, second flush, an excellent tea for important occasions.

Pandam, FTGFOP1, first flush, an early evening tea.

Puttabong, FTGFOP1, first flush, sublime afternoon tea.

Puttabong, FTGFOP1, second flush, a great tea, perfect for the afternoon.

Risheehat, FTGFOP1, second flush, a first-class, daytime tea.

Seeyok, GFOP, first flush, the five o'clock tea par excellence.

Seeyok, FTGFOP, in between, the perfect beverage for five o'clock tea.

Selimbong, GFOP, second flush, an excellent, refreshing tea.

Singbulli, GFOP, second flush, an afternoon tea that can tolerate a splash of milk.

Singtom, FTGFOP, first flush, a subtle, daytime tea.

Teesta Valley, TGFOP, second flush, perfect for brunch.

Tumsong, GFOP, first flush, a large estate, a tea with a balanced taste

TERAI
Black teas from the northern plains of India, generally used to enhance certain blends, except for some estates.

Ashapur, CTC.

Kamala, CTC.

Ord, TGFOP, a morning tea.

Pahargoomiah, CTC.

DOOARS
Black teas from the northern plains of India, generally used to enhance certain blends, except for some estates.

Bhatpara, CTC.

Good Hope, TGFOP, a daytime tea.

Toonbarie, CTC.

Soongachi, CTC.

NILGIRI
Pungent black teas from the high plateaus in the south of India.

Nilgiri, BOP, daytime teas.

Nunsuch, TGFOP, daytime teas.

CEYLON (Sri Lanka)

BLACK TEAS
Six great regions producing full-flavoured teas that suit the European palate. The high grown, (high altitude) teas are the best – the low grown, are more ordinary.

DIMBULA
(high grown)

Dyagama, BOP, major estate, pronounced flavour, stands a drop of milk.

Dimbula, BOP, one of the top estates, a morning tea.

Kenilworth, OP1, a great tea at any time.

Loinorn, Pekoe, superb flavour, strong, a morning tea.

Pettiagalla, OP1, exceptional afternoon tea.

Radella, BOP, an excellent morning tea.

Somerset, Pekoe, strong and full flavoured, a morning tea.

Theresia, BOP, renowned estate, a morning tea.

GALLE
(low grown)

Allen Valley, FOP, a five o'clock tea.

Berubeula, OP1, less rare than the FOP, perfect for five o'clock tea.

Devonia, FOP, vintage, a late afternoon tea to accompany food.

Galaboda, OP1, perfect for brunch.

NUWARA ELIYA
(high grown)

Maha Gastotte, BOP, a morning tea.

Nuwara Eliya, OP, one of the finest Ceylon teas, to be enjoyed in the afternoon.

Tommagong, BOPF, a fortifying morning tea.

RATNAPURA

(low grown)

Ratnapura, OP, a five o'clock tea.

UVA
(high grown)
Aislaby, BOP, an outstanding estate, a pungent breakfast tea.

Attempettia, FP, famous, a strong tea for any time of day.

*Dyraaba,*BOPF, so strong it could be a substitute for coffee.

Roehampton, BOP, strong tea, tolerates a dash of milk.

*Saint James,*OP, famous tea, to be enjoyed at any time of day.

Saint James, Fannings the finest on the island, a tea for any time of day.

Uva Highlands, FP, a morning tea.

DECAFFEINATED TEAS
There are many excellent teas in FP, BOP and OP.

JAPAN

Japan only produces green teas, which can be drunk at any time of day and can accompany meals.

Bancha, bright tea, of middling quality, slightly bitter.

Fuji-Yama, tea of exceptional quality, aromatic.

Genmaicha, a blend of *Sencha* or *Bancha* with toasted rice or maize, giving a unique taste.

Gyokuro, a precious and refined tea from the first crop only, grown in the shade.

Matcha, powdered tea (*Gyokuro* or *Tencha*) also makes delicious iced tea.

Sencha, bright tea, the most popular in Japan.

Sencha Honyama, excellent morning tea, very aromatic, acts as a tonic.

Sencha Ariake, daytime tea, subtle, with a rich bouquet.

Tamaryokucha, refreshing tea suitable for any time of day.

Tencha, a tea grown in the shade, from the first and second crop, mild and light.

INDONESIA

Tea produced in Indonesia is of medium quality and is usually used in tea bags. There are, however, some very good estates that produce top-quality black teas with rich flavours.

Malabar, OP, famous estate in Java, an afternoon tea.

Taloon, GFOP, one of Java's main estates, a subtle afternoon tea.

VIETNAM

Small-scale production of black, lightly flavoured teas, slightly fermented teas, green teas and jasmine teas.

Annam, Pekoe, black tea with a hint of spice, a morning tea.

GEORGIA

The Russian tea for samovars above all others, small-scale production of medium quality.

Georgia, OP, a mild, evening tea.

TURKEY

Large-scale production for domestic consumption. Also makes tea for samovars.

Rize, BOP, full-flavoured morning tea.

Rize, OP, mild evening tea.

KENYA

Leading African producer of tea of consistent quality, 99 per cent is in the form of CTC.

Highgrown, Pekoe, full-flavoured morning tea from the high plateaus.

Marinyn, GFOP, extensive Kenyan estate, a refreshing tea for any time of day.

BLENDS

Nine classics which can be excellent if they are made from good quality teas.

Afternoon Tea, made of an Assam or African tea and a Ceylon Nilgiri or a Darjeeling, it is less strong and more aromatic. To be drunk later in the day, as the name indicates.

Brunch, made from an Assam and a Darjeeling, a balanced tea that can accompany meals.

*Caravan,*made from unsmoked China teas, low in caffeine, with lots of flavour.

Chine pointes blanches, made of smoked and non-smoked China teas with downy buds. An unusual tea.

English Breakfast, same blend as for Afternoon Tea, but with BOP instead of FOP, full-flavoured tea for the English breakfast.

Five O'Clock Tea, FOP or OP, made from a Ceylon and a Darjeeling or Assam, a delicate tea to be drunk at five o'clock.

Irish Breakfast, made from a Ceylon and an Assam, a scented, full-flavoured tea for breakfast time.

English Blend, can be made from Indian, African, Chinese, Argentinian or Ceylon teas – so everything depends on the individual blend and the quality of the teas.

Imperial or, made from Chinese teas, one lightly smoked, the other jasmine. Delicate flavour.

Each major tea house has its own blends. Give them a try.

SCENTED TEAS

The classic scented teas are Earl Grey (scented with bergamot), jasmine teas, and traditional scented teas such as chrysanthemum, orange flower, lychee, lotus flower, magnolia (Yulan Huacha), and rose (Meigui Hongcha). Teas can also be scented with flowers, citrus fruits, exotic fruits, and traditional fruits. The important thing is that the flavours are natural and not artificial.

Handy uses for tea

A cleaning agent

When brewed and left to go cold, tea can be used to clean mirrors, chrome and wooden panelling. Chinese Buddhist monks make the most of its grease-dissolving properties and use the brewed leaves to clean their plates.

A deodorising agent

If you buy a clay dish and it has an unpleasant smell, try boiling some tea leaves in it for a few hours, or if any of your cooking utensils, such as frying pans, have retained the smell of fish, you can rub them with tea leaves that have been brewed and drained, but are still wet. It's also useful for getting rid of the smell of onions from your hands! The Chinese, experts on the deodorising qualities of tea, fill little bags with dried tea leaves and place them in cupboards, toilets and shoes. What's more, tea has antibacterial properties. Burning the leaves can freshen and purify the air in a room.

Cooking

When soaking dried fish, add some brewed tea leaves to the water to prevent the loss of proteins .

The garden

Brewed leaves mixed with soil make an excellent fertiliser for plants.

Skin care

Green tea reduces redness and soothes sensitive skin. It can be used in a compress on the eyes to relieve pressure and is even said to add shine to dull brown hair.

How to remove tea stains

If the stain is old, rub it with glycerine mixed with water. On white fabric, soak the affected area with a few drops of lemon juice and wash in cold water. On coloured cloth, soak the material in an egg yolk mixed with lukewarm water. To clean a carpet or rug, use a mixture of one part methylated spirits and one part dry white wine or white vinegar. Pour over the affected area and press firmly with a dry cloth.

How much do you know?

1 • What is the difference between a black tea leaf and a green tea leaf?

2 • Tea is good for your teeth. True or false?

3 • Does Assam tea come from China or India?

4 • Does the region of Darjeeling have 87 or 1,200 estates?

5 • How many species of tea plant are there?

6 • Orange Pekoe is a tea scented with orange. True or false?

7 • Which country is the world's biggest producer of tea?

8 • Lapsang Souchong is the most popular tea in China. True or false?

9 • What does Darjeeling mean?

10 • Bergamot is a mixture of spices. True or false?

11 • Is Matcha a China tea or a Ceylon tea?

12 • Where are bricks still the preferred form in which to make tea?

13 • Matcha is a tea that has been reduced to a powder. True or false?

14 • Tea was one of the causes of the American War of Independence. True or false?

15 • What did Ceylon produce before it became a major tea producer?

16 • Which tea is more highly smoked – Tarry or Lapsang Souchong?

17 • What does the word 'Samovar' mean?

18 • What do the Chinese call black tea?

19 • Is Earl Grey a tea blend, a scented tea, or a tea that has been harvested early?

20 • Opium was used as an exchange currency for tea in the 19th century. True or false?

21 • Is mint tea made with Darjeeling or Yunnan?

22 • Do the Tibetans add salt, butter or onion to their tea?

23 • Are vitamins found in the upper or lower leaves of the tea plant?

24 • Who was responsible for the code of the tea ceremony – Sen No Rikyû or Lu Yu Sen?

25 • Is tap water good for making tea?

26 • Orange Pekoe means 'little orange leaf'. True or false?

27 • It was the Trans-Siberian Railway that put an end to the tea caravans. True or false?

28 • Was the clipper originally an English or an American boat?

29 • The French grew tea plants in Brittany. True or false?

30 • What is a zhong?

ANSWERS

1. Black tea leaves are fermented and green are not.
2. True. Even if it stains teeth yellow, it is very rich in fluoride (particularly green tea) and prevents tooth decay.
3. India.
4. 87.
5. A single species but many varieties.
6. False. It's a grade of tea that is produced from a high-quality but late crop.
7. India, which produces 750,000 tonnes (738,000 tons) of tea, followed by China, which produces 600,000 tonnes (590,400 tons) of which 403,000 tonnes (396,550) are green tea.
8. False. It is a smoked tea, usually reserved for exportation.
9. 'Place of thunderbolts' in Tibetan.
10. False. It is a citrus fruit resulting from the hybridisation of a lemon tree and a bigarade tree (a type of orange tree).
11. Neither. It's a green tea from Japan.
12. Tibet.
13. True. It's a Tencha, reduced to a powder then whisked. It is used in the tea ceremony.
14. True. The first hostilities date back to the Boston Tea Party in 1773, when the settlers threw 342 cases of British tea into the sea.
15. Coffee. This product made the island rich from 1825 until the plantations were devastated by rust between 1865 and 1890.
16. Tarry Souchong. The Taiwanese varieties are more highly smoked than the Chinese ones.
17. 'Samo' means 'by itself' and 'varit' means 'boil'.
18. Red tea. The name is derived from the colour of the liquid not the leaf.
19. It's a tea scented with bergamot.
20. True. It was introduced to China by the English (who imported it from India) and was the cause of two wars between the two powers (1840–42 and 1856–60).
21. Neither. It's made with a Chinese green tea, usually Gunpowder.
22. They add all three.
23. In the upper leaves.
24. Sen No Rikyû, grand tea master in the 16th century.
25. Tap water may have been treated with chlorine or other chemicals, so spring or mineral water is better if it is available.
26. False. Orange comes from the Oranje Nassau family, one of the first importers of Dutch tea.
27. True. The railway only took a few days to transport tea between China and Russia, whereas the caravans took six months to reach the border town of Nijni-Novgorod.
28. American.
29. True. Or at least, they tried. Their attempts weren't very successful: the region of Finistère was certainly wet, but it was too cold.
30. A zhong is a cup with a lid and deep saucer but no handle.

Films

THE TEAHOUSE OF THE AUGUST MOON

American film by Daniel Mann (1956), produced by Jack Cummings/MGM.
The US Army attempts to Americanise a tiny Okinawan village following the second World War. Instead of building a school, however, the Japanese prefer a tea house.

UGETSU MONOGATARI

Japanese film by Kenji Mizoguchi (1953), produced by Masaichi Nagata/Daiei.
Tea in ancient Japan.

LE THÉ À LA MENTHE

French film by Abdelkrim Bahloul (1984), produced by Enterprise Française de Production.
Tea – a link between immigrants and policemen.

THE BITTER TEA OF GENERAL YEN

American film by Frank Capra (1932), produced by Walter Wanger/Columbia Pictures Corporation.
Tea in the confrontation between East and West in China.

EAT A BOWL OF TEA

American film by Wayne Wang (1989), produced by American Playhouse Theatrical/Columbia.
Chinese immigrants come to terms with life in New York's Chinatown in the immediate post-war years.

DEATH OF A TEA MASTER
(Sen No Rikyu)

Japanese film by Kei Kumai (1989).
In 1618, two men endeavour to understand why the famous tea master, Sen No Rikyu, committed harikiri 17 years previously. Magnificent adaptation of the novel by Yasushi Inoue.

THE WIND WILL CARRY US
(Bad ma ra khahad bord)

Iranian film by Abbas Kiarostami (1999), produced by Marin Karmitz and Abbas Kiarostami/MK2.
In a village in Iranian Kurdistan, a man from Tehran never takes time to drink his tea.

HOWARDS END

British film by James Ivory (1981), produced by Ismail Merchant.
Features an example of tea-drinking in Victorian England.

TEA AND SYMPATHY

America film by Vincente Minnelli (1956), produced by Pandro Berman/MGM.
Secrets are confided and attachments formed over a cup of tea.

THE LADY VANISHES

British film by Alfred Hitchcock (1938), produced by Edward Black/Gainsborough Pictures.
A very special tea bag is first a clue, and then proof.

THE SHELTERING SKY

Italian film by Bernado Bertolucci (1990), produced by William Aldrich and Jeremy Thomas.
Tea and the Sahara are a mirage for New Yorkers trying to escape from their problems.

TEA WITH MUSSOLINI

Anglo-Italian film by Franco Zefirelli (1999), produced by Cineritmo, Cattleya, and Medusa Produzione.
A cup of tea in Fascist Italy in the 1930s.

TOKYO STORY

(Tokyo Monogatari)
Japanese film by Yasujiro Ozu (1953), produced by Shochiku/Ofuma.
Tea in modern Japan.

Further reading

Best Tea Places in Britain, The Tea Council, 2000.

Jennifer L Anderson, *An introduction to Japanese Tea Ritual, State University of New York Press, Albany, NY,* 1991.

John Blofeld, *The Chinese Art of Tea, Shambhala Publications Inc,* 1997.

Lewis Carroll, *Alice's Adventures in Wonderland, Oxford Paperbacks,* 1998.

Victoria Dolby, *All About Green Tea, Avery Publishing Group.*

Anton Edelmann, *Taking Tea at the Savoy, Pavilion Books,* 1999.

Julie Fisher, *Coffee and Tea Lover's Cookbook, Sunset Books.*

Clare Gordon-Smith, *Teatime, Ryland, Peters and Small,* 2000.

Geraldene Holt, *A Cup of Tea, Pavilion,* 1991.

James Joyce, *Ulysses, Oxford Paperbacks,* 1998.

Okakura Kakusô, *The Book of Tea, (original edition, New York,* 1906*), Tuttle Publishing,* 2000.

Kenneth Kiple and Kriemhild Conee Ornelas, eds, *Tea in The Cambridge History of World Food, Cambridge University Press,* 2000.

Elizabeth Knight, *Tea with Friends, Storey Communications,* 1998.

Robert Laxalt, *A Cup of Tea in Pamplona, University of Nevada Press,* 1992.

Sandy Lynam Clough, *With a Cup of Tea, Harvest House Publishers,* 1997.

Lesley Mackley, *Afternoon Tea, Salamander,* 1992.

Rosemary Moon and Jane Suthering, *Fortnum and Mason, A Fine Tradition of Tea, In Triplicate/Good Books,* 1998.

Dominique T. Pasqualini, *Le Temps du thé, Marval,* 1999.

Marguerite Patten, *Complete Book of Teas, Piatkus,* 1996.

Alexander Pushkin, *Eugene Onegin, Penguin,* 1999.

Marcel Proust, *Swann's Way, Vintage,* 1996.

Diana Rosen, *Chai: the Spice Tea of India.*

Helen Simpson, *The London Ritz Book of Afternoon Tea: The Art and Pleasure of Taking Tea, Morrow, William & Co,* 1998.

Margaret Thornby, *Margaret Thornby's guide to Tea Rooms of Britain, Whithall Publishing,* 1998.

Kim Waller, *The Pleasures of Tea: Recipes and Rituals, Morrow, William & Co,* 1999.

Robert Wemischner, *Diana Rosen Cooking with Tea: Techniques and Recipes for Appetizers, Entrées, Desserts, and More, Periplus Éditions,* 2000.

Where to buy tea

Wherever you are in the UK, and indeed throughout the world, you are unlikely to be far from a good tea supplier. Many types of tea can now be bought from supermarkets though for a specialist tea you may still have to visit a specialist supplier.

LONDON

FORTNUM AND MASON
181 Piccadilly
London W1A 1ER
Tel: 020 7734 8040
www.fortnumandmason. co.uk

HARRODS LTD
87 – 135 Brompton Road
Knightsbridge
London SW1X 7XL
Tel: 020 7730 1234

SELFRIDGES
400 Oxford Street
London
W1A 1AB
Tel: 020 7629 1234
www.selfridges.com

HARVEY NICHOLS
109-125 Knightsbridge
London
SW1X 7RJ
Tel: 020 7235 5000
www.harveynichols.com

THE DRURY TEA AND COFFEE COMPANY
37 Drury Lane
Covent Garden
London
WC2B 51A
Tel: 020 7836 1960

TWININGS
216 Strand
London WC2
Tel: 020 7353 3511

WHITTARD OF CHELSEA
203–205 Brompton Road
Knightsbridge
London SW3 1LA
Tel: 020 7591 0148
(Branches also in Covent Garden, Carnaby Street Hampstead High Street High Street Kensington and Richmond)

OUTSIDE LONDON

BETTYS OF HARROGATE
Parliament Square
Harrogate
North Yorkshire HG1 2QU
Tel: 01423 502746
www.bettysbypost.com
(Branches also in Ilkley, Northallerton and York)

WHITTARD OF CHELSEA HAS MANY BRANCHES THROUGHOUT THE UNITED KINGDOM, A COMPLETE LIST CAN BE FOUND AT
www.whittard.com/shops uk

ROYAL WINDSOR TEA COMPANY BERKSHIRE
www.webworld.co.uk

PARIS

MARIAGE FRÈRES
30, rue du Bourg-Tibourg
75004 Paris
Tel: 0033 1 42 72 28 11
13, rue des Grands-Augustins
Tel: 0033 1 40 51 82 50.
260, rue du Faubourg-Saint-Honoré
75008 Paris
Tel: 0033 1 42 65 86 17
www.mariagefreres.com

BETJEMAN AND BARTON
23, boulevard Malesherbes
75008 Paris
Tel: 0033 1 42 65 86 17
www.betjeman@wanadoo. fr

KUSMI (RUSSIAN TEAS)
75, Avenue de Niel
75017 Paris.
Tel: 0033 1 42 27 91 46

LA MAISON DE LA CHINE
76, rue Bonaparte
75006 Paris
Tel: 0033 1 40 51 95 00
www.maisondelachine.fr

NEW YORK

ABC PARLOUR CAFÉ
88 Broadway
New York

TAKASHIMAYA
693, Fifth Avenue, New York
Tel: 001 212 753 20 38

BOSTON

REBECCA'S CAFÉ
75 State Street, Boston, MA.
Tel: 001 617 261 00 22
(Branches also in High Street, Newbury Street, Tremont Street and Boylston Street)

JAPAN

MARIAGE FRÈRES OSAKA
2-1-17 Shinsaibashi-Suji
Chuo-Ku
Tel: 0081 06 62136575

LE PALAIS DES THÉS
5-24-2 Okusawa Setagaya
Tokyo.

TEA CEREMONIES

URASENKA
4 Langton Way
London
SE3 7TL
Tel: 020 8853 2595
A branch of the largest tea school in Japan, which teaches the tea ceremony.

Tea rooms

LONDON

THE CONSERVATORY AT THE LANESBOROUGH
Hyde Park Corner
London SW1X 7TA
Tel: 020 7259 5599

THE DORCHESTER
54 Park Lane
London W1A 2HJ
Tel: 020 7629 8888
www.dorchesterhotel.com
Tea served 2.30 – 6 pm daily.

THE RITZ
Piccadilly
London W1
Tel: 020 7493 8181
Tea served 2.30 – 6 pm daily.

THE SAVOY HOTEL
Strand
London WC2
Tel: 020 7836 4343
Tea served 3 – 5.30 pm daily.
Tea dance, Sundays.

CLARIDGES
Brook Street
London W1
Tel: 020 7629 8860
Tea served 3 – 5.30 pm daily.

WALDORF MERIDIEN
Aldwych
London Wc2
Tel: 020 7836 2400
Tea served 3 – 5.30 pm
Monday to Friday.
Tea dance, Saturdays.

FORTNUM AND MASON
181 Piccadilly
London W1
Tel: 020 7734 8040
www.fortnumandmason.
co.uk

THE FOUR SEASONS
Hamilton Place,
Park Lane, London W1A 1AZ
Tel: 020 7499 0888.

THE TEA HOUSE
College Farm
45 Fitzalan Road
London N3 3PG
Tel: 020 7240 9571

EAST ANGLIA

THE CAKE TABLE TEA ROOM
5 Fishmarket Street
Thaxted, Essex CM6 2PG
Tel: 01371 831206

TEA ON THE GREEN
3 Eves Corner
Danbury
Essex CM3 4QF
Tel: 01245 226616

THE TEA AND COFFEE HOUSE
6–7 Market Place
Hitchin
Hertfordshire SG5 1DR.
Tel: 01462 433631.

MARGARET'S TEA ROOMS
Chestnut Farmhouse
The Street
Baconsthorpe
Norfolk NR25 6AB
Tel: 01263 577614

FLYING FIFTEENS
19a the Esplanade
Lowestoft
Suffolk NR33 0QG.
Tel: 01502 581188.

THE MIDLANDS

THE MARSHMALLOW
High Street
Morton-in-Marsh
Gloucestershire
Tel: 01608 651536

THE OLD SCHOOL TEA ROOM
Carburton
Near Worksop
Nottinghamshire S80 3BP
Tel: 01909 483517

OLLERTON WATERMILL TEA SHOP
Market Place
Ollerton
Newark
Tel: 01623 824094/822469

BENSON'S OF STRATFORD-UPON-AVON
4 Bards Walk
Straford-upon-Avon
Warwickshire CV37 6EY.
Tel: 01789 261116

NORTHERN IRELAND

BEWLEY'S CAFÉ AND SHOP
Rosemary Street
Donegall Arcade
Belfast BT1 1PT
Tel: 048 90 234955

THE NORTH-EAST

BETTYS CAFÉ TEA ROOM
1 Parliament Square
Harrogate
North Yorkshire HG1 2QU
Tel: 01423 502746

32–34 The Grove
Ilkley
West Yorkshire LS29 9EE
Tel: 01943 608029

188 High Street
Northallerton
North Yorkshire DL7 8LF
Tel: 01609 775154

6–8 St Helen's Square
York
North Yorkshire YO1 2QP
Tel: 01904 659142
www.bettysbypost.com

CRATHORNE HALL HOTEL
Near Yarm
North Yorkshire TS15 0AR
Tel: 01642 700398

THE NORTH-WEST

HAZLEMERE CAFÉ AND BAKERY
1 Yewbarrow Terrace
Grange-over-Sands
Tel: 01539 532972

THE COTTAGE TEA ROOM
3 Fennel Street
Ashford-in-the-Water
Near Bakewell
Derbyshire DE45 1QF
Tel: 01629 812488

NOSTALGIA TEAROOMS
215-217 Lord Street
Southport
Lancashire PR8 1NZ
Tel: 01704 501294

GREYSTONES 17TH CENTURY TEA ROOMS
Stockwell Street
Leek
Staffordshire ST13 6DH
Tel: 01538 398522

SCOTLAND

ABBEY COTTAGE TEA ROOMS
26 Main Street
New Abbey
Dumfries
DG2 8BY
Tel: 01387 850377

THE CALEDONIAN HOTEL
Princes Street
Edinburgh EH1 2AB
Tel: 0131 4 599988

KIND KYTTOCK'S KITCHEN
Cross Wynd
Falkland
Fife KY15 7B
Tel: 01337 857477

THE SOUTH-EAST

PAVILLION TEA ROOMS
Royal Parade
Eastbourne, East Sussex
BN21 7AQ
Tel: 01323 410374

CLARIS'S
1 High Street
Battle
East Sussex TN33 OAE
Tel: 01424 772314

HASKETT'S TEA AND COFFEE SHOP
86 South Street
Dorking
Surrey RH4 2EW
Tel: 01306 885833

THE SOUTH-WEST

THE OLD RECTORY FARM TEAROOMS
Rectory Farm
Morwenstow
Near Bude
Cornwall
EX23 9SRR.
Tel: 01288 331251

THE COMMODORE HOTEL
Marine Parade
Instow
Devon EX39 4JN
Tel: 01271 860347

COURT BARN COUNTRY HOUSE HOTEL
Court Barn Country House Hotel
Clawton
Holsworthy Devon
EX22 6PS
Tel: 01409 271219.

THE BRIDGE TEA ROOMS
24a Bridge Street
Bradford-on-Avon
Wiltshire BA15 1BY
Tel: 01225 865537

POLLY TEA ROOMS
26-27 High Street
Marlborough
Wiltshire SN8 1LW
Tel: 01672 512146

WALES

BADGERS
The Victoria Shopping Mall,
Mostyn Street, Llandudno
LL30 2RP
Tel: 01288 331251

THE ST TUDNO HOTEL
Promenade, Llandudno,
Gwuynedd LL30 2LP
Tel: 01492 874411

EIRE

BEWLEY'S ORIENTAL CAFE
10/12 Westmoreland Street
Dublin 2
Tel: 00 353 1 6776761

BEWLEY'S CAFÉ
78 Grafton Street,
Dublin 2
Tel: 00 353 1 6776761

BEWLEY'S CAFÉ
4 Cook Street
Cork
Tel: 00 353 21 4270660

BEWLEY'S CAFÉ
Cruises Street
Limerick
Tel: 00 353 61 414739

(Branches also in Ennis,
Kilkenny and Waterford)

PARIS

AUX DÉLICES DE SCOTT
*39, avenue de Villiers
75017 Paris
Tel: 0033 1 47 63 71 36*

BROCCO
*180 rue du Temple
75003 Paris
Tel: 0033 142 72 19 81*

MARIAGE FRÈRES LE MARAIS
*30, rue du Bourg-Tibourg
75004 Paris
Tel: 0033 1 42 72 28 11*

PRIORI THÉ
*35-37, passage Vivienne
75002 Paris
Tel: 0033 1 42 97 48 75*

TEA CADDY
*14 rue St.Julien -au- Pauvre
75005 Paris
Tel: 0033 1 43 54 15 56*

AMSTERDAM

CAFÉ FRANÇOISE
*The mists of the North and
the aromas of tea.
Kerkstraat 176, Amsterdam*

MONTREAL

SALON DE THÉ CAMELLIA SINENSIS
*351, rue Emery, Montreal
Tel: 001 514 286 40 02*

MOSCOW

CAFÉ MARGARITA
*Malaïa Bronnaïa Oulitsa 28
Moscow*

NEW YORK

TAKASHIMAYA
*693, Fifth Avenue, New York
Tel: 001 212 753 20 38*

TEA & SYMPATHY
*108 Greenwich Avenue
(at 13th Street)
New York
Tel: 001 212 807 8329*

PRAGUE

PLHA CAFÉ
*Wide selection of teas
served in an art gallery.
Klimentska and Revolucni,
Prague 1*

DOBRA CAJOVNA
*Tea shop in the Staré Mesto
district serving a wide
range of teas.
Václavské nam 14, Prague 1*

ROME

BABINGTON'S TEA ROOMS
Piazza di Spagna, 23, Rome

SEOUL

YET CHA CHIP
*A tea house in the district of
calligraphers and antique
dealers (Sa Dong). Plays
Buddhist music and birds
fly above you while you sip
your tea.
2–2 Kwan Hun Dong
Chong Ro-Gu, Seoul*

VIENNA

HEINER
*Vollzeile 9,
Kärntner Strasse 21-23
Vienna*

Glossary

ANHUI
Province of central China, one of the main producers of black and green tea.

ASSAM
Province of north-east India producing a tea of the same name.

BANCHA
Medium-quality Japanese green tea.

BANKING
Liquid retained by a drained leaf after brewing, only released if pressed with your fingers.

BLACK (TEA)
Fermented tea.

BLEND
Mixture of different teas.

BROKEN
Tea made from leaves that are broken during rolling.

BROKEN ORANGE PEKOE (BOP)
Grade of black tea characterised by even, broken leaves from a fine crop.

BROKEN PEKOE (BP)
Grade of black tea characterised by the broken second and third leaves, stronger than the BOP.

CAMELLIA
Botanical genus of the tea plant.

CEYLON
Former name of Sri Lanka. The name 'Ceylon' was preserved to denote the teas produced on this island.

CHA
'Tea' in Chinese.

CHAIRI
Basin for heating tea.

CHANOYU
Name given to the Japanese tea ceremony, literally 'hot water for tea'.

CHINGWOO
Black unsmoked China tea from the plantations in the province of Fujian.

CHUNG
Chinese tea cup with no handle but a lid and a deep saucer.

CHUN MEE
Green tea whose leaf is rolled lengthways.

CLIPPER
Fast sailing boat used during British supremacy to transport tea from Asia to Europe.

CONGOU
A black China tea.

CROP
Term used in China instead of flush (India) to denote a harvest (first crop, second crop).

CTC
Crushing, tearing, and curling. One of the processes in the production of black tea.

DARJEELING
Mountainous province in the north of India producing tea of the same name.

DIMBULA
Region of Sri Lanka producing strong, pungent teas.

DOOARS
Province in the north of India producing a tea of the same name.

DRYING

One of the stages in the production of tea during which the leaves are dried.

DUST

Tea that has been reduced to dust, generally used in tea bags.

EARL GREY

Blend of unsmoked teas scented with bergamot.

ESTATE

Tea plantation, also called 'garden'.

FACTORY

Place where tea is manufactured.

FANNINGS

The broken leaves of black tea, between 1 mm (0.04 in) and 1.5 mm (0.06 in) in size.

FERMENTATION

One of the stages in tea production.

FINE PLUCK

A fine harvest.

FINEST TIPPY GOLDEN FLOWERY ORANGE PEKOE (FTGFOP)

Flowery Orange Pekoe of exceptional quality.

FIRST FLUSH

Used in India to designate the first harvest of the year (mainly for Darjeeling teas). The leaves are plucked between 15 March and 15 May.

PEKOE

Grade of black tea characterised by leaves between 5 mm (0.2 in) and 8 mm (0.3 in) in size, rolled lengthways.

FLOWERY PEKOE (FP)

Grade of black tea characterised by whole leaves rolled into a ball obtained from fine plucking.

FUJIAN

Tea-producing province of China.

GALLE

Region in Sri Lanka producing a Ceylon tea.

GENMAICHA

Blend of green tea (Bancha or Sencha), maize and toasted rice. Japanese speciality.

GOLDEN BROKEN ORANGE PEKOE (GBOP)

Grade of tea which is Broken Orange Pekoe with golden tips.

GOLDEN FLOWERY ORANGE PEKOE (GFOP)

Grade of tea which is Flowery Orange Pekoe with golden tips.

GOLDEN TIPS

The gold-coloured tips or buds of certain leaves in black tea. A highly sought-after feature.

GRADE

Quality of a tea determined by how much the leaf is broken (whole, broken, or dust).

GREEN (TEA)

Non-fermented tea.

GUANGXI

Tea-producing province of China.

GUIZHOU

Tea-producing province of China.

GUNPOWDER

Green tea, usually from China, made of young leaves plucked in April and rolled into little balls.

GYOKURO

Means 'dewdrop' in Japanese. High-quality tea that spends part of its cultivation time in the shade.

HARDENING OFF

The process of gradually exposing a tree nursery to the sun to allow the young tea plants to become accustomed to it.

HIGH GROWN

High-altitude tea and tea plantation (above 1,200 metres, 3,900 feet).

HUBEI

Tea-producing province of China.

HUNAN

Tea-producing province of China.

HYSON

Means 'flowery spring' in Chinese. Green tea.

ICHIBAN-CHA

Japanese word used to describe the 'first tea' or 'first crop'.

IMPERIAL (CROP)

Crop in which the bud or the bud and one leaf (P+1) is plucked.

INDIAMEN

Slow, heavy boats that transported tea for the East India Company, eventually superseded by the clippers.

INFUSION

The wet leaves left over after preparing a tea.

KABUSE-CHA

Tea plant grown in the shade in Japan.

KANDY

Region in Sri Lanka producing Ceylon tea.

KEEMUN

Black tea from China, native to the province of Anhui.

LAPSANG SOUCHONG

Smoked black China tea from the province of Fujian.

LOW GROWN

Low-altitude tea and tea plantation (below 600 metres, 2,000 feet).

MATCHA

Powdered green tea used in the Japanese tea ceremony.

MEDIUM PRUNING

Type of pruning used to trim down the trees to a manageable level and regenerate the tea plant.

MID GROWN

Mid-altitude tea and tea plantation (between 600–1,200 metres, 2,000–3,900 feet).

MUSCATEL FLAVOUR

Highly sought-after flavour of the Muscat grape, a characteristic of certain second flush Darjeeling teas.

NATURAL LEAF

Tea leaves in their natural state – whole leaves that have been neither rolled nor smoked.

NIGHT SHADOW

Japanese green tea from the province of Shizuoka.

NILGIRI

Region in south-east India producing teas of the same name.

NINGCHOW

China tea from the province of Hubei.

NURSERY

Tree nursery.

OOLONG

Means 'black dragon' in Chinese. Semi-fermented tea from China, mainly Taiwan (Formosa).

ORANGE PEKOE (OP)

Grade of black tea characterised by large leaves between 8 mm (0.3 in) and 15 mm (0.6 in), rolled lengthways.

PAI MU TAN

One of the two varieties of white tea.

PANYONG

Black China tea from the province of Fujian.

PEKOE (P)

Means 'white down, or hair' in Chinese. Grade of black tea characterised by whole leaves rolled into a ball, larger than the Flowery Pekoe.

PEKOE CONGOU

Black tea from southern China.

PEKOE SOUCHONG (PS)

Grade of black tea characterised by whole leaves rolled into a ball from a coarse crop (third leaf).

PINGSUEY

Green China tea from the province of Zhejiang.

PLUCKING

Harvesting the tea leaves.

POUCHONG

A lightly fermented Oolong tea, mainly from Taiwan.

PRUNING

Trimming the tea plant.

QUALITY TEAS

Teas harvested in a good-quality season.

RAIN TEA

Teas harvested in the monsoon season.

RED (TEA)

Fermented tea.

ROLLING

One of the stages of tea production.

RUST

Disease found on tea and coffee plants.

SAMBA-CHA

Means 'third tea' or 'third crop' in Japanese.

SANCHUN

Means 'third leap' or 'third crop' in Chinese.

SECOND FLUSH

Term used in India to describe the second crop of the year (mainly for Darjeeling teas). The leaves are plucked between 15 June and 15 August.

SEMI-FERMENTED (TEA)

Oolong teas have the scent of green teas and the flavour of black tea.

SENCHA
Japanese term for 'natural leaf' describing an ordinary green tea.

SHOOT
Plucked shoot.

SILVER TIPS
Silver-coloured tips or buds of certain leaves used in black tea.

SOUCHONG (S)
Last grade of black tea meaning 'subvariety' in Chinese and referring to the large mature leaves.

SPRING TEAS
Teas produced from the spring harvest.

STALKS
Pieces of stalk found in some teas made from a coarse crop.

SUMMER TEAS
Teas produced from the summer harvest.

SICHUAN
Black China tea from the province of Sichuan.

TARRY SOUCHONG
Very highly smoked black tea.

TERAI
Region in the north of India, south of Darjeeling, producing teas of the same name.

TIPPY GOLDEN FLOWERY ORANGE PEKOE (TGFOP)
Flowery Orange Pekoe with many golden tips.

UVA
Region in Sri Lanka producing rounded, mellow teas, not as strong as Ceylon tea.

WHITE (TEA)
A rare tea from a bush with white leaves grown in the province of Fujan in China.

YELLOW (TEA)
A variant of green tea.

YIN ZHEN
One of the two varieties of white tea.

YUNNAN
Province of China producing teas of the same name.

ZHEJIANG
Province of China producing teas of the same name.

ZHONG
Cup with a lid and deep saucer used in China.

Contents

Fact ⟫ 2–10
Fun facts and quick quotes

Discover ⟫ 11–32

Look ⟫ 33–54
Sharing a cup, bowl or mug of tea at different latitudes

In Practice ⟫ 55–102

Find out ⟫ 103–125

Credits

P. 12, 14, 16, Mariage Frères – **P. 19,** Tea House, Japanese print, Musée des arts asiatiques-Guimet, RMN (J. L'hoïr) – **P. 21,** English tea in le Salon des quatre glaces at the palais du Temple in Paris in 1764, painting by M.-B. Ollivier (1712-1784), Versailles, RMN – **P. 22,** Gathering of Russian folk, end of 19thC., Jean-Loup Charmet – **P.24,** The Boston Tea Party, 1846, Currier & Ives, The Bridgeman Art Library – **P. 27,** Le Thermopylae, J. Gardner, Le Chasse-Marée – **P. 29,** Library of the Maisons-Alfort vetinary school at Selva – **P. 30,** Mariage Frères – **P. 34-35,** Vu (Matthieu Ricard) – **P. 36,** Magnum (René Burri) – **P. 37,** Gamma (Jeremy Horner) – **P. 38,** Magnum (Harry Gruyaert) – **P. 39,** Métis (Max Pam) – **P. 40-41,** Hoaqui (Richer) – **P. 42,** Vu (Bernard Descamps) – **P. 43,** Hoaqui (E. Valentin) – **P. 44-45,** Fotogram-stone (Bushnell/Soifer) – **P. 46,** Magnum (Raymond Depardon) – **P. 47,** Cosmos (W. Gartung) – **P. 48-49,** Magnum (Paul Lowe) – **P. 50,** Magnum (Peter Marlow) – **P. 51,** Cosmos (A. Boulat) – **P. 52-53,** Hoaqui (V. Durruty) – **P. 54,** Vu (J.-E. Atwood) – **P. 55,** Mariage Frères – **P. 56-57,** Christophe Chalier – **P. 58,** Bios (Alain Compost) – **P. 59,** Christophe Chalier – **P. 60-61,** Christophe Chalier, Mariage Frères (Jean-Pierre Dieterlen) – **P. 62-65,** Christine Fleurent for the bowls, Phare international (G. Nencioli), for the teas – **P. 66-69,** Phare international (G. Nencioli) – **P. 70,** Mariage Frères – **P. 71,** Christine Fleurent, Christophe Chalier – **P. 72,** Gamma (Xu Bang) – **P. 73,** Christophe Chalier, Mariage Frères for the tin – **P. 74-75,** Christophe Chalier – **P. 76,** Explorer (J. Wishnetsky) – **P. 77,** Christophe Chalier – **P. 78,** Explorer (C. Boisvieux) – **P. 79, 80,** Christophe Chalier – **P. 82,** Bodum, Christophe Chalier – **P. 83,** Mariage Frères – **P. 85,** Bodum, Christophe Chalier – **P. 86-89,** Phare international (G. Nencioli) – **P. 91,** Christine Fleurent, Christophe Chalier – **P. 93-94-97-98,** – **P. 101-102,** Saveurs (Pierre Desgrieux).

Acknowledgements

The authors would like to thank Guy Fillion and Élisabeth Van Egroo.
The editor would like to thank the following: Mariage Frères for their kind co-operation, Pi design for Bodum, Geneviève Lethu, 60 rue de Sablonville, 92200 Neuilly and La Compagnie française de l'Orient et de la Chine for their help with the documentation.